Integrating Web Services with OAuth and PHP

by
Matthew Frost

A™ a php[architect] guide

Integrating Web Services with OAuth and PHP

First Edition: February 2016
ISBN - Print: 978-1-940111-26-1
ISBN - PDF: 978-1-940111-27-8
ISBN - ePub: 978-1-940111-29-2
ISBN - Mobi: 978-1-940111-28-5
ISBN - Safari: 978-1-940111-30-8
Produced & Printed in the United States

Disclaimer

Written by
Matthew Frost

Published by
musketeers.me, LLC. 201 Adams Ave.
Alexandria, VA 22301 USA

240-348-5PHP (240-348-5747)

info@phparch.com
www.phparch.com

Editor-in-Chief
Oscar Merida

Managing Editor
Eli White

Technical Reviewer
Oscar Merida

Copy Editor
Kara Ferguson

Layout and Design
Kevin Bruce

For everyone who's helped me along the way, especially Chris Hartjes, Matt Turland, Yitzchok Wilroth, Beth Tucker Long, Tyler Etters, Nick Escobedo, and Jeff Carouth.

Table of Contents

Table of Contents

Foreword

"Any sufficiently advanced technology is indistinguishable from magic."

Arthur C. Clarke

I became a Facebook user back when it was still exclusive to college students, before it became a platform for third-party applications. Not long after I graduated, I also became an early adopter of Twitter. This was in the days before OAuth, when the API used Basic HTTP authentication and many users would provide their username and password to third parties to try out the latest new app or client. Those were simpler times with a naïve and yet blissful ignorance about them.

I still remember using dial-up internet for the first time and being amazed at the possibilities of a world-wide network when I'd only ever seen a few machines wired together to play games over a local area network. The Internet has grown up a great deal since then, and we've had to grow with it. Once we got over the excitement of our new found ability to share information and the vast possibilities that lay therein, a critical realization followed: we also needed the ability to protect our information from those who would use it for less than noble purposes.

This grew ever more important as applications continued to evolve and increase in complexity, to the point where they would be used to identify us to third parties and share our information with them. At that point, we needed the ability to selectively grant those third parties access to our information without giving up the proverbial keys to the kingdom: our account credentials.

All it took was one nefarious or even innocently misbehaving app to wreak havoc with your account. You could reset your password, of course, but that would revoke access to your account for all other apps you used. HTTP authentication was no longer sufficient for the purposes of applications in this situation. A better solution was needed, and Twitter led the charge with OAuth 1 when it became a published standard in 2010.

While it paved the way forward for a standard to solve this class of problem, OAuth 1 had its drawbacks. The signature process it used in lieu of SSL was complex and made writing clients cumbersome. It lacked workflows for applications beyond those involving communication between two web applications, such as desktop and mobile. OAuth 2 would succeed it only two years later after the issues with it became apparent.

In the midst of all these technological developments, I had the good fortune to become acquainted with Matt Frost through the PHP community and the PHP Mentoring program. We began our relationship as mentor and apprentice, but became friends and even co-workers at one point.

I've believed for some time that everyone is in a position to be both a student and a teacher to others. Matt has proven that by writing this book and reversing the nature of our original relationship to make me the student, as the book's subject has been one that I've personally struggled with since OAuth first became a standard.

I hope you'll follow me in allowing the words that Matt has written to dispel the magic that may surround OAuth for you as it has for me. While you continue to witness the evolution of the internet and all its technological wonders, I hope you will also be mindful of how it can best benefit humankind.

Matthew Turland
New Orleans, LA
June 24, 2014

Foreword

Chapter

1

HTTP Basics

It's no secret the Internet is everywhere; it powers a large amount of the software we use every single day. An explosion of Application Programming Interfaces (APIs) has significantly increased the number of different services that can be integrated into a single piece of software. In spite of these obvious observations, one thing has remained constant: HTTP (HyperText Transfer Protocol) is the backbone of the Internet. Since the days when browsers were rendering sparkly star backgrounds underneath a myriad of randomly placed images, HTTP has been the protocol responsible for serving up (thankfully, not creating) these web pages.

In order to build applications which are responsive and useful for the end user, it's important to understand HTTP and the structure of the requests, as well as the responses they generate. Though it may seem trivial for static web sites and applications with minimal functionality, in today's world of highly integrated web applications understanding the protocol is a necessity. An understanding of HTTP allows other systems and developers to interact with our code in a logical way and accelerates the development process. HTTP is a collection of rules for transferring text, images, videos, and sounds in addition to other file and data types across the web via the transmission of requests and responses. Much like linguistic communication, a browser or server will request a specific resource from a web server; the request will also provide specific details to ensure the response can be delivered the way the requesting server expects. The server receiving the request will attempt to act on the specific details of the request and will report back to the requestor whether or not their request could be fulfilled and return any pertinent information regarding the request. That's a pretty high level overview of how HTTP generally works; if you would like more detail you can read through the HTTP/1.1 RFC [1].

This chapter will focus on the very basics of HTTP. It is not intended to be an exhaustive resource on the topic, but should provide enough information to gain a better understanding of how OAuth works in the context of an application.

The Problems with Authentication

We all interact with authentication and authorization on a daily basis. In fact, most of the time it has nothing to do with the code you write or the applications you use. If you have a keypad on your garage, a swipe card to enter the office, or a debit card with a Personal Identification Number (PIN) then you are constantly authorizing transactions and actions. We are also aware of the risks and precautions we need to take to ensure that information isn't disseminated. Losing your swipe card, debit card, or PIN can lead to unauthorized users gaining access to your finances or place of employment. Your garage code can lead to your house being vandalized, burgled, or worse. We treat these scenarios as serious security breaches, as we should. If we're smart, our PIN isn't the same as our garage code and doesn't contain any other personal information that can be used to gain access to other systems.

We have the same risks and should be taking equally effective precautions with interacting with applications on the internet. As more of our daily lives have moved online we appreciate the convenience, but don't always consider the legitimate security risks (or the impact) breaches can have on our professional and personal lives. What it comes to down to is being as certain as possible that when our online accounts, application accounts and residential security systems authorize access, we're the person initiating those requests. Imagine the outrage if your bank made your PIN available through relatively little effort. As application developers, we need to take great care to ensure the authorizing information our users trust us with is effectively protected.

Most applications these days require you to login with a user name and password. It's more common than not for users to have accounts on multiple web sites providing a myriad of different services. Some applications have leveraged this fact and allow you to login with credentials from popular services like Facebook, Twitter, and GitHub–to name a few. While this is usually quite convenient, it should make us wonder "Am I giving my Facebook credentials to another website?"

By now we know this isn't the case. We see this when we are redirected to the Facebook or Twitter login page to enter our credentials and we understand the results of our authentication attempts are then communicated back to the application we are trying to use. Without this service to handle the interactions between services, it becomes very insecure for two applications to interact with each other.

[1]   http://phpa.me/http11-rfc2616

It's important to understand this point because it helps to understand the role OAuth fills in our modern day web fueled world. One of the largest fears is that somehow our credentials will be sent across the internet in plain-text. Plain-text information is easily captured by hackers; if our personal password practices are sloppy, this can open anyone up to a world of professional, financial, and even personal pain. You might be wondering who would pass plain-text credentials across the internet in an unencrypted manner. All it takes is one application getting sloppy with your personal information and the havoc mentioned above is right around the corner.

As responsible web developers, we rely on HTTP requests to deliver enough information in the request to properly identify a user (authentication) and allow the application to determine whether the user has access to the requested resource (authorization). When you break it down, developers are responsible for so many difficult things end users take for granted. There is an expectation that other users will not be able to make requests on their behalf, that their user name and password will be properly protected, and that they will be able access everything they have permission to access. No matter your experience level, these are difficult problems and require a great deal of thought and planning to address.

Breaking Down HTTP Requests/Responses

HTTP requests and response can provide a great deal of information to developers allowing us to create secure, personalized experiences for the users of our application. This includes everything from learning whether our requests were successful, to learning what browser or utility is being used to make the request. By learning how these requests are formatted, what content is available and how to access them in PHP, we unlock valuable information for our application.

Requests

The response shown below is an example of the Headers sent as part of the request. As you can see, the request specifies the format and encoding it expects to receive from the response. It also specifically mentions the host and path where the requestor believes the resource is located.

```
GET /Protocols/rfc2616/rfc2616.txt HTTP/1.1
User-Agent: HTTPie/0.9.2
Host: www.w3.org
Connection: keep-alive
Accept: */*
Accept-Encoding: gzip, deflate
```

The response shown below will indicate whether a resource was found on the host and path indicated in the request and will include some additional information about the response. The status code offers a quick, specific update on whether or not the request was successful. It also indicates the format of the response, the length of the response, and some cache information like the last time the page was edited, the date and time of the request, and a date and time for when the results of this request expire.

```
HTTP/1.1 200 OK
Date: Fri, 18 Dec 2015 04:15:45 GMT
Server: Apache/2
Last-Modified: Tue, 29 Jul 2008 15:34:19 GMT
ETag: "69810-4532b5f92d4c0"
Accept-Ranges: bytes
Content-Length: 432144
Cache-Control: max-age=21600
Expires: Fri, 18 Dec 2015 10:15:45 GMT
P3P: policyref="http://www.w3.org/2014/08/p3p.xml"
Content-Type: text/plain
```

In the examples above, it's important to note the headers are sent in plain-text and each header is terminated by a carriage return and new line character (\r\n). It is possible to inspect these headers in Chrome and Firefox by right clicking on the page and selecting *Inspect Element*. This will open up the browsers development tools. Once the window opens on the bottom, the *Network* tab will allow you to see all the HTTP requests that were made to render the page. Clicking on any single request will reveal information about the request, including the Request and Response headers. You can also download browser extensions to directly craft and inspect HTTP requests.

Requests are messages sent from the client to the server and give the server enough information to carry out an action on the supplied resource. The resource is identified by a URI, or Uniform Resource Indicator. A URI has a couple of components: the protocol, the host, and the path. A URL, or Uniform Resource Locator, is a type of URI and has the following format:

`{protocol}://{host}{path}{query:optional}{port:optional}`

You'll notice there are place holders for query and port, both of those components aren't required to form a valid URI. A default port for the specified protocol will be used if it is missing, for HTTP it is port 80. Query is completely optional. The client must provide the server with the resource, the data for the resource, and the action the server should attempt. There are many tools we use everyday that will abstract this step away, for example, a web browser. With a web browser, we provide the resource we'd like the server to retrieve and display for us. We don't necessarily need to know we're asking the server to perform a GET action on the resource, but that's exactly what happens.

While providing the action and resource isn't overly complicated, it makes sense to take a quick look at how this is formatted.

`GET http://facebook.com HTTP/1.1`

By looking at this request, one can readily determine what the client is asking the server to do. We're sending a request to http://facebook.com and asking the server to *get* or *retrieve* the resource located at http://facebook.com. If you notice, the HTTP version is also being sent along with the action and the resource. This is explicitly telling the server what version of HTTP to use. Finally, each header in the request is terminated by a CRLF (carriage return line feed). A later section in this chapter will delve into more specific information about the actions a server can understand and how those actions operate.

While the header above will make the request to facebook.com and retrieve the resource, there are other headers that can be sent to protect us, and ensure we only get back the type of resources we expect. Some of these are very important, especially when dealing with unfamiliar APIs, but it's usually a good practice to include them in any case. I have provided more information on some of these useful headers in the next section.

Useful Headers

Accept:

The Accept header tells the server what type of resource the client is willing to accept in the response. This can be very important to ensure the data sent back from the server is not overtly malicious, or unable to be displayed properly by the client. For example, when interacting with an API where the response is expected to be returned in JSON (JavaScript Object Notation), setting the Accept header to application/json will ensure if the response is not JSON, that it will not be returned. Here is an example of a request sent with the Accept header:

```
GET http://somecoolapi.com/v1/user/1b1c3fe76a HTTP/1.1
Accept: application/json
```

Accept-Charset

The Accept-Charset header tells the server what character set the client is willing to accept in the response. It is important to understand what the server is sending back and how different character sets might work or not work with your application. It is possible for the server to send back a different character set than you might expect, so if your application is displaying data from the response you should know how to request specific character sets from the server. Here is an example of a request sent with the Accept-Charset header:

```
GET http://somecoolapi.com/v1/user/1b1c3fe76a HTTP/1.1
Accept-charset: utf-8
```

Host

The Host header is required with every request and is used to identify the host the request is trying to reach. This header allows allows the request to be sent as a relative path the to the host, though the full resource path can still be sent as well. The Host header will assume the request is being sent to port 80, but a different port can be specified as well. If for some reason, the request does not have an internet host, the header must be sent with an empty value. Here is an example of a request sent with the Host header and a relative path:

```
GET /v1/user/1b1c3fe76a HTTP/1.1
Host: http://example.com
```

It's worth noting this is by no means an exhaustive list, for more information on the types of headers that can be sent with the request take a look at the HTTP 1.1 RFC (RFC-2616).

Response

Once the server receives the request, it attempts to fulfill the request and responds to the client with the results of the request. In the same way that the headers are descriptive of the request, the response sends headers describing the results of the request. As you might expect, a successful request indicates the server was able to locate the resource and perform the specified action on the resource. A request can fail for a number of reasons; it's possible the resource couldn't be found, the request wasn't formatted properly, or the client doesn't have permission to access the resource. Every request has a status code corresponding to result of the request; they are universally used and understood.

The response gives the client the opportunity to respond to the failure in an appropriate way. For example, in the web browser a request to a missing resource could generate a 404 page. When making a request to a web service it can be used to craft a message in a web environment, throw an Exception, or create a log entry for the errant request. To gain an understanding of how to analyze the HTTP response we'll look at a few common, meaningful headers as well as how to set server specific headers.

Response Headers

Status Code

The status code is included with every response and its purpose is to communicate whether the request has successful and if not, why it failed. Status codes are a component of the protocol and do not change from server to server, which allows their meanings to be universally understood. The status-line in the response provides the status code and a phrase describing the code. It's relatively simple, but here is an example of a status line for a successful request:

```
200 OK
```

Content-Type

The Content-Type header communicates the content type of the data being returned in the body of the response. When the request specifies an Accepts header, the Content-Type header should match one of the provided values in the request. Here is an example of what the Content-Type header would look like when JSON is returned:

```
Content-Type: application/json
```

Content-Length

The Content-Length header communicates the size of the content in the body, in terms of number of bytes. This header prevents you from having to make function calls to figure out the length of the response body. Here is an example of the Content-Length header:

```
Content-Length: 9720
```

X-* Type Headers

Any header prefixed with X- is a custom header being used to communicate application or service specific information. This is commonly used with APIs to communicate the rate limit and how many requests have been used against the rate limit. These headers can contain anything the server wishes to communicate back to the client. Here's an example of the rate limit headers from the Twitter API:

```
X-Rate-Limit-Limit: 150
X-Rate-Limit-Remaining: 130
```

Response Body

The response body is the content returned in response and is formatted based on the content type. If we look at our example of the web browser, the content body would be the HTML content the user would expect to see. This is what the user will actually be consuming, while the headers provide information about the response and the body.

Stateless Nature of HTTP

HTTP is stateless, which means every single request is independent of any other requests. Once a login request is processed, HTTP no longer knows anything about the request. It has no idea if the previous request was successful, if a new request is from the same user, or even if the user was logged in. This, of course, requires any state maintenance to be handled by the developer outside of HTTP. To handle this developers often use cookies, sessions, databases, or caching tools. The state retrieved from those tools would need to be explicitly sent with each HTTP request or the application would have to prevent the request from being made if the user is in the incorrect state.

When a user logs into a web application, an HTTP request is made to a resource to ensure the provided credentials match a user in the system. From that point onward the application "remembers" the user is logged in. Imagine if the user had to login to an email system and then re-enter their credentials before opening every email; it would be hard to imagine that email service (or any other service) convincing people to use their site. It's a pretty ridiculous scenario, right? This is exactly what HTTP requires.

> By State *we mean an application remembers some details about a client from one request to the next.*

The concept is really quite straight-forward, HTTP operates independently of your application or DSL (Domain Specific Language) and won't understand what "logged in" or "authorized" means in the context of the application. Understanding this also helps you develop intelligently and securely; by trying to make HTTP do something it's not meant to do, we can put our users' data at risk.

Verbs and Statuses

If you read the previous section, you read some references to "actions" or HTTP verbs and statuses. Verbs are used by the client to communicate what action the server should take on the resource. Statuses are codes that correspond to phrases to communicate whether or not the request was successful. There are number of statuses which provide a detailed explanation of what happened with the request. These two concepts are very important in understanding how to interact with web services.

Verbs

While there are a handful of verbs, we're going to take a look at a few of the most commonly used verbs and explain what they mean in the context of HTTP.

- GET: The GET verb is a means of retrieving information from the Request-URI. In the cases where the endpoint creates or produces data, the GET request will only return the data being produced. When there is a need to pass parameters to the endpoint, these are passed through a query string. In the endpoint www.example.com/index.php?id=1&group_id=5, the query string starts at the ? character and contains everything to the right of that character (?id=1&group_id=5 in this specific case). The values in the query string are a key/value pair separated by an =. Multiple pairs are separated with a & or & .

- POST: The POST verb is intended as a way to create a new resource on the server. This is commonly used in web forms to send the form data to the server where it will be stored. The server defines the means in which the data will be stored and the verb is used as a method of informing the server it should execute the storage process. Parameters for a POST request are not appended to the Request-URI, but are instead sent over as POST fields.

- PUT: The PUT verb is used as a method to update an existing resource on the server. For example, when a user fills out a registration form to create their account on the server they are using a POST request. However, if any part of that user's data changes (they get a new phone number perhaps), the modification should happen with a PUT request.

- DELETE: The DELETE verb is perhaps the most descriptive of the verbs, in the sense it is intended to remove a resource from the server. As in the other requests, the server is responsible for the implementation of the delete, whether that means actually removing it, or moving it to an inaccessible location.

Status Codes

Status codes are three digit codes paired with a phrase explaining whether or not the status completed successfully. The first digit in each three digit code corresponds to a category of statuses. Typically, by looking at the first digit a user can tell whether the response is providing information (100); was successful (200); has been redirected (300); there was an error in the request (400); or there was an error on the server (500). Generally speaking, there is nothing a client can do about a status code in the 500 range; however, with 400 codes the status code can provide information so the client can change/fix their request.

Provided below is a list of status codes and their phrases. The status codes themselves are self-explanatory, but this list should give you an idea of the type of information you can get from the status codes and phrases.

Informational (100)

These indicate a provisional response. They are not supported by HTTP/1.0, because that version of the protocol did not define 1xx codes.

- 100 Continue
- 101 Switching Protocols

Success (200)

A 2xx code indicates the server successfully received, understood, and accepted the client request.

- 200 OK
- 201 Created
- 202 Accepted
- 203 Non-Authoritative Information
- 204 No Content
- 205 Reset Content
- 206 Partial Content

Redirection (300)

Servers use this class of code to indicate to a client further action needs to be taken to fulfill the original request.

- 300 Multiple Choices
- 301 Moved Permanently
- 302 Found
- 303 See Other
- 304 Not Modified
- 305 Use Proxy
- 307 Temporary Redirect

Client Error (400)

This set of status codes are meant to indicate the client made some sort of error in their request, such as being malformed or not allowed.

- 400 Bad Request
- 401 Unauthorized
- 402 Payment Required
- 403 Forbidden

- 404 Not Found
- 405 Method Not Allowed
- 406 Not Acceptable
- 407 Proxy Authentication Required
- 408 Request Time-out
- 409 Conflict
- 410 Gone
- 411 Length Required
- 412 Precondition Failed
- 413 Request Entity Too Large
- 414 Request-URI Too Large
- 415 Unsupported Media Type
- 416 Requested Range Not Satisfiable
- 417 Expectation Failed

Server Error (500)

A complement to 400 level errors, this status code indicates the server encountered some unexpected condition and could not fulfill the client's request.

- 500 Internal Server Error
- 501 Not Implemented
- 502 Bad Gateway
- 503 Service Unavailable
- 504 Gateway Time-out
- 505 HTTP Version not supported

While there are certainly more topics that could be covered on HTTP, understanding these concepts will help the remainder of the material make sense. Since OAuth very heavily relies on being able to send headers and understand responses correctly, this material is a great start on the quest to understanding OAuth more completely.

Chapter 2

Introduction to OAuth

The Internet has become so diverse with tools and applications we often run into the problem of connecting them together. Applications now collaborate and share information like never before, giving users a better experience and a more powerful online presence. This chapter is going to discuss how OAuth connects these services together without putting your personal information at risk.

Challenges of Authorization and Authentication

Authorization and authentication are difficult promises to solve in software and one of the most fundamental expectations users have when using an application. It's reasonable to expect other users will not be able to see private portions of your account, create unauthorized content with your account, or take any other sort of action without your knowledge As software developers, we try to guide our users into simple steps to protect themselves from other users gaining access to their account, but as we know, it doesn't always work. Bear in mind, right now we're discussing a single user in a single system and haven't even scratched the surface of how one user is going to safely integrate multiple accounts. As you can see, this is a very important challenge to overcome.

Before we go any further, we need to define a couple of key terms used throughout the book. The two main concepts of a site that has user accounts is ensure users can log in, and to ensure users can only operate in ways allowed by the application. We're going to look at these two concepts in greater detail right now.

Authentication

If we really think about the act of a user logging into a system, we expect the user will identify themselves using key pieces of information only they (hopefully) know. Commonly this is a *password*. Authentication is the process by a which a user verifies their identity to gain access to a system. Though the processes of logging in and having access to all the appropriate information are seamless to the user, they are really completely separate. Authentication allows the application to verify the user exists in the system, nothing more. The authentication process allows access to the application, but doesn't specify what resources the user is able to see or modify. Only after the user's identity is confirmed, can we determine what the user is allowed to access.

Consider a business that requires the use of badges to gain admittance to the building. If an employee shows up and swipes their badge, they are identified as an employee of the company and able to gain access. In the same way, a valid username and password identifies a user in an online application. There are other resources within the building which certain individuals may or may not have access to, like the supply closet or a server room. Simply being an employee of the company doesn't grant them access to these protected resources, it merely identifies the user as someone who works for the company.

Authorization

Authorization determines whether or not the identified user has access to a certain resource or set of resources. If we operate under the assumption users can only post content from their own user account, authorization is the step which prevents user "joesmith" from posting a status or an update as "janedoe". With authorization, we already have an authenticated user and know who we are dealing with before we make any determination to whether the action being attempted is allowed.

If we go back to the previous real world example, using our badge to gain access to the building doesn't necessarily give us access to all the resources in the building. If an employee belongs to a group of employees which has access to a supply closet or server room, the same identification badge can be used to gain access. The important difference is of course, the specific user has permission to enter the room, where as, others do not. This concept is sometimes known as Access Control, but it is the same process of specifically restricting people from accessing resources or rooms.

More Challenges

In a web application, we often notice we are only required to log into the system once, until our identification expires and we must re-identify. This is because web applications have the ability to maintain a specific application state. An application requiring a user to log in every time they wanted to go to a different resource or page within the application would be quickly discarded as unusable. As applications grow and require more integrations from outside systems, this process becomes more complicated.

If you are like me, you don't want to provide your username and password for one application to a completely different application. If there were a security breach on another service, the attackers would quickly be able to gain access to other accounts you own, and the potential damage they could cause is much greater. We also know we don't want another service to login to another service for us, and we trust there is a secure method of retrieving information that doesn't expose our secret identification. Because of this, the use and production of APIs has grown tremendously in order to integrate two completely different systems.

The other large problem we run into is when we are accessing information from another service, we're doing so in stateless manner. This means when we allow a service, for example Facebook, to access our Twitter account, neither Facebook nor Twitter are keeping track of the fact at some point we logged into the other system. This means every time we make a request for a resource, we need some way to authenticate ourselves and allow the service to determine if we are authorized to access a resource.

This section provides more questions than it does answers and that's alright; we're going to get into how OAuth solves these problems a little later in the chapter. For now, it's important you understand the difference between authorization and authentication and how they are used in the context of an application.

Differences Between OAuth 1 and 2

As with any piece of software, when enough enhancements become obvious new versions spring to life adding useful features and removing features which are no longer needed. In this regard, OAuth is no different; while you can still find services supporting OAuth version 1, version 2 was created to correct some of the issues presented in version 1. This section will detail what some of these changes are without diving into all the technical details. It is important to understand the differences between the two, specifically if you are considering an OAuth implementation for your business or service.

Signatures

OAuth signatures are used, as you might imagine, to sign the requests you're making to the API. This signature is one of the main components necessary to identify the user making the request. OAuth version 1 had very stringent requirements when it came to the signature, including sorting the elements in authorization header alphabetically and encoding the signature before sending it. OAuth version 2 does not rely on generated signatures to identify the user, though the user must pass along an access token in place of the signature. The simplified method of authenticating removes the need to parse, sort, and generate individual signature components.

Short-lived Tokens

Tokens are used in OAuth to identify a user and are generated when the user grants permission for another application to use his or her data. Tokens serve as a substitute for passing usernames and passwords in the request and unlike usernames and passwords can be revoked and regenerated at any time. OAuth 1 provides tokens which are available for a long period of time to ensure the user doesn't have to continually regenerate new tokens. As with username and password combinations, tokens that exist for a long time are less secure because they are tied to the same entity for a long time. OAuth 2 provides the ability to generate short-lived access tokens which shorten the amount of time an individual token is tied to a specific user. In addition to the short-lived token, there is also a long-lived refresh token which allows the tokens to be regenerated after they expire, and doesn't require the user to regenerate the tokens themselves.

Bearer Tokens

OAuth 2 provides the ability to generate *Bearer Tokens*, which are able to be used without cryptography. They are sent over HTTPS and serve to identify a user without the need to generate a signature. This tends to be a commonly used method of authentication in OAuth and was not available in OAuth 1. They do not provide any additional security outside of the protocol they are transported by, which should always be SSL.

This is a quick look at some of the changes and differences between OAuth versions 1 and 2. These concepts will be covered in greater detail in the corresponding chapters.

When Do I Need a Client/Server

As we start to get a deeper understanding of OAuth, authentication, and authorization in general, we need to decide what types of OAuth components we need to implement it in our application. OAuth has both client and server specifications and they serve very different purposes. It is important to understand the roles and functions of the both components when designing an application or API.

Client

The term *Client* indicates this component will be making requests to obtain or alter information on another system. Typically, a client application will read and manipulate data from another service. The sole responsibility of the client is to create the requests and provide the proper identification of the user that wishes to make them, to ensure the user exists, and the action is permissible. If your application is going to be consuming or altering data on a third party system using OAuth for authentication, you will need to provide an OAuth Client capable of creating and signing the requests in a way the server will understand. That is to say, if the third party service is using an OAuth 2 server, the requests must be formatted to fit the OAuth 2 specifications. In that case, you will need an OAuth 2 client. In a system interacting with multiple third-party sources, it is possible you will need to provide a client for each version and idiosyncratic implementations of OAuth so the properly formatted requests can be made to each source.

For example, when Twitter first became popular, it allowed many different client applications to fetch a user's stream, post updates, and send messages.

Server

The term *Server* indicates this component will be receiving the requests from a client. The server is the application which has resources clients want to fetch and interact with. The server must verify any request is signed properly and handle the authorization component of the request as well. The server will attempt to identify the user making the request, ensure that they are authorized to make such a request, and verify the resource being requested actually exists.

In the event the user is identified and authorized for the action they are attempting to make, the server will then allow the action to be carried out and return a response. The response is broken up into two different components: the response headers and the response body. If the request was successful, the body is the content being requested; otherwise, it generally contains a specific error message explaining why the request failed. The headers also give a good deal of information about the request, including the content type, status and length of the content. Status codes are universally understood and eliminate the need for each API to develop its own error code system. By sticking with HTTP status codes, you can clearly communicate the status of the requests with almost any user in the world.

In Chapter 1, we covered HTTP Status codes. These are used to communicate to the client whether the request was successful. If your application will be providing an API and you intend to use OAuth to handle authorization and authentication, you will need to provide an OAuth Server to handle the requests that are being sent by the client.

Conclusion

As you can see, it is possible for an application to require both the use of an OAuth server and an OAuth client in order to meet the needs of the application. The chapters covering the client and server implementations for each version of OAuth will provide far more technical detail. As you start to design your application, it is important to understand the differences between the client and server, and how to determine whether you will need either or both to meet your needs.

Solving Auth Challenges with OAuth

We've covered the difficulties of authentication and authorization with APIs in some detail. It makes sense to discuss a few ways OAuth helps solve some of these challenges. The most difficult balance we have to achieve is between security and usability. OAuth, while not perfect, helps us bridge the gap and provide a secure authentication process that's easy for the end user to consume.

Repeated Auth

We've discussed briefly when consuming APIs we expect the environment to be stateless, because communication take place over HTTP. This means the API is not going to remember a specific client previously authenticated. By definition, this requires a user to be authenticated and authorized for every single request. You already know how quickly users would flee your application if they had to provide a username and password for every request made (keep in mind some pages make multiple requests).

OAuth handles this repeated authorization process with tokens and signatures and—with the exception of Bearer Tokens in OAuth 2—requires every request be signed appropriately. A token identifies a user as an authenticated account on a third party service without exposing the user's login credentials. When authorizing access from a third party, a user will generally log into the third party website and access tokens are generated to identify the user on other systems. With these tokens, the application can build the proper signature (which will be discussed in greater detail in later chapters) and request information from the third party service. The configuration of the service usually requires these tokens be provided once so each request can be signed without the need to continually provide the tokens. The tokens can be regenerated or revoked on the third party website at any time, which is often less time consuming than resetting a password and adds an additional layer of security.

Security

We know sending our credentials in a raw, or unencrypted, format is dangerous because it increases the probability they can be stolen from a request by anyone who can read the contents of the request. The opportunity for having our username and password stolen increases with every request we send. Regardless of how we authorize and authenticate, it's important to use SSL to transport credentials so the data is not sent across the Internet in a human readable format. It's also important to keep the SSL certificates current and updated. With that disclaimer out of the way, let's take a look at how OAuth provides a higher level of security than other methods.

If we were to use our username and password to authenticate every request, we'd be required to send them with every single request. Since the basic expectation of the user would be to provide the credentials once per session, we would also expect the client application we were using to store those credentials. As we've seen from some very public and embarrassing revelations in the recent past, even large reputable companies don't always take care of our credentials the way they ought to. One example might be storing passwords with a one-way hash. Obviously, providing a username and password to any other entity opens us up to our credentials being misused. Or worse yet, the potential situation also exists where the entity is hacked and credentials for various external applications are obtained with malicious intent. At this point, we're left to hope and trust our information is stored in a secure manner. If companies don't secure credentials to their own applications, it's silly to expect them to secure the credentials for applications which integrate with theirs. It only takes one hack or one disclosure for sensitive data to be obtained and for people's lives to be potentially ruined.

The use of tokens is very important to OAuth as it allows a secure way for users to be identified. If an application were to be hacked and this data exposed it would take a matter of minutes for the tokens to be regenerated rendering any unauthorized attempts fruitless. Tokens are usually generated in pairs, there are tokens which identify the application as well as the user. There is a public token that can be viewed by looking through the HTTP headers, but the private token is used to build the signature and without it, the requests cannot be properly signed. It's the very reason the user is informed to not share the secret token with anyone else when they're generated.

OAuth also requires the use of a nonce to protect against replay attacks. In simple terms, a replay attack is when an attacker eavesdrops on a client server transaction and attempts to resend the transaction. A nonce is an arbitrarily generated number that can only be used once. A request using the same nonce twice in a predetermined amount of time will be rejected. This prevents the same request from being made repeatedly and generally relies on the authentication method to create the nonce with every request.

As you can see, OAuth was designed with these concerns in mind and strikes a good balance between security and user experience. While OAuth certainly helps us make good, safe decisions it is still very important to utilize defensive programming to limit the vulnerability of your application. Your application can still be vulnerable to many other attacks, even if you use OAuth. Don't be lulled into a false sense of security your application is safe. Work to ensure every aspect of your application or API is reasonably protected against all types of attacks.

Removing the Magic

The term *magic* is generally used when a software component works and the developers working with it can't easily understand how. Magic is never a good thing; when decisions are made and improperly abstracted, debugging becomes nearly impossible. For a lot of people OAuth seems like magic, in large part because it's a completely different authentication model than people are accustomed to using. While there is a learning a curve, it is still very important to understand how the components of an OAuth request are generated.

Some of the concepts are unfamiliar. To ensure we are not relying on software that isn't understood by the developers, we have to really break down what the code is doing and how it's producing these results. Removing the magic isn't an attempt to rewrite or re-engineer; it's an attempt to understand the core of the code to ensure we don't get burned in the future.

Using Existing Libraries is Good

The best code is the code you never had to write, and in the PHP world it's becoming easier and easier to find packages and libraries capable of providing much of the functionality you would have to write otherwise. The same is true for OAuth, the purpose of this book is **not** to encourage you to write your own OAuth implementation library, but to more fully understand what the libraries you are using are doing for you. Widely used libraries have already gone through a vetting process where major bugs can be found and remedied. Essentially, all the work has been done for you. Good libraries have also been used by many other developers and have the reputation of being reliable. By avoiding *Not Invented Here* syndrome or NIH, it's possible to understand what the library is doing in a very granular way and redirect the use of your time to writing the components and features your application requires. While I'm not suggesting people write their own OAuth implementations, understanding how it works also provides opportunities to contribute to existing libraries.

Nothing is perfect, but what is important is the code we are writing solves the problem it was intended to solve. Your users won't care if you wrote your own OAuth implementation, but they will care considerably more if your implementation misses the mark and exposes them to vulnerabilities and annoying breaks in functionality. Technology moves and changes quickly; having an understanding of the underlying technology can put you in a position to contribute heavily when things change. If you really have an interest in writing an implementation, consider contributing to Open Source libraries to improve their code and documentation.

Decoupling Auth

Hopefully we all strive to write small modules of code which can be used together and reused. How many auth implementations are tied directly to the application using it? Significant changes in the data store or how the application operates shouldn't require significant changes in other areas of unrelated code. The term coupling refers to how closely connected different components in our application are relative to each other. Tightly coupled applications generally exhibit a behavior of cascading changes. Or more simply put, when you make a change to a module of code many other changes must be made to separate modules for the application to function correctly.

By using OAuth, we get started down the right path of loose coupling. We know our Authentication process is going to be singularly focused and we'll be able to easily drop this protocol in place in our application. The key is to be able to ensure the Auth process knows as little about the application as possible to do its job. By using tried and tested libraries, we can ensure our Auth process stays out of the way of the rest of our application, which will allow us to maintain functionality without a major headache or support burden.

Chapter
3

OAuth 1 Client

Our deep dive into the functionality of OAuth will begin by looking at the client for OAuth 1. The term *client* has a lot of different contexts, but in this context we're referring to any program able to make a valid OAuth request. The client has the responsibility of first properly identifying the user trying to request a protected resource. Since we're using OAuth to avoid having to pass our credentials around the Internet, it's important to understand verifying an identity is more complex than a simple username/password combination.

Learning how to make OAuth requests allows you to interact with more services and build a more robust, integrated user experience in your application. If you are planning to build an API, understanding how the requests are made will give you valuable insight on what to look for when validating them. This chapter is going to focus on some of the core concepts in building an OAuth request, namely, the signature, the nonce, and tokens. Figure 3.1 shows the flow of requests in OAuth 1.0.

Components of an OAuth 1 Signature

As you've seen in the preceding chapters, we will use HTTP Headers to identify our clients to a server. Before proceeding, you should be familiar with the concepts in Chapter 1, specifically with how HTTP Headers work. While that chapter will not make you an HTTP expert, it provides enough information and concepts needed to understand this chapter.

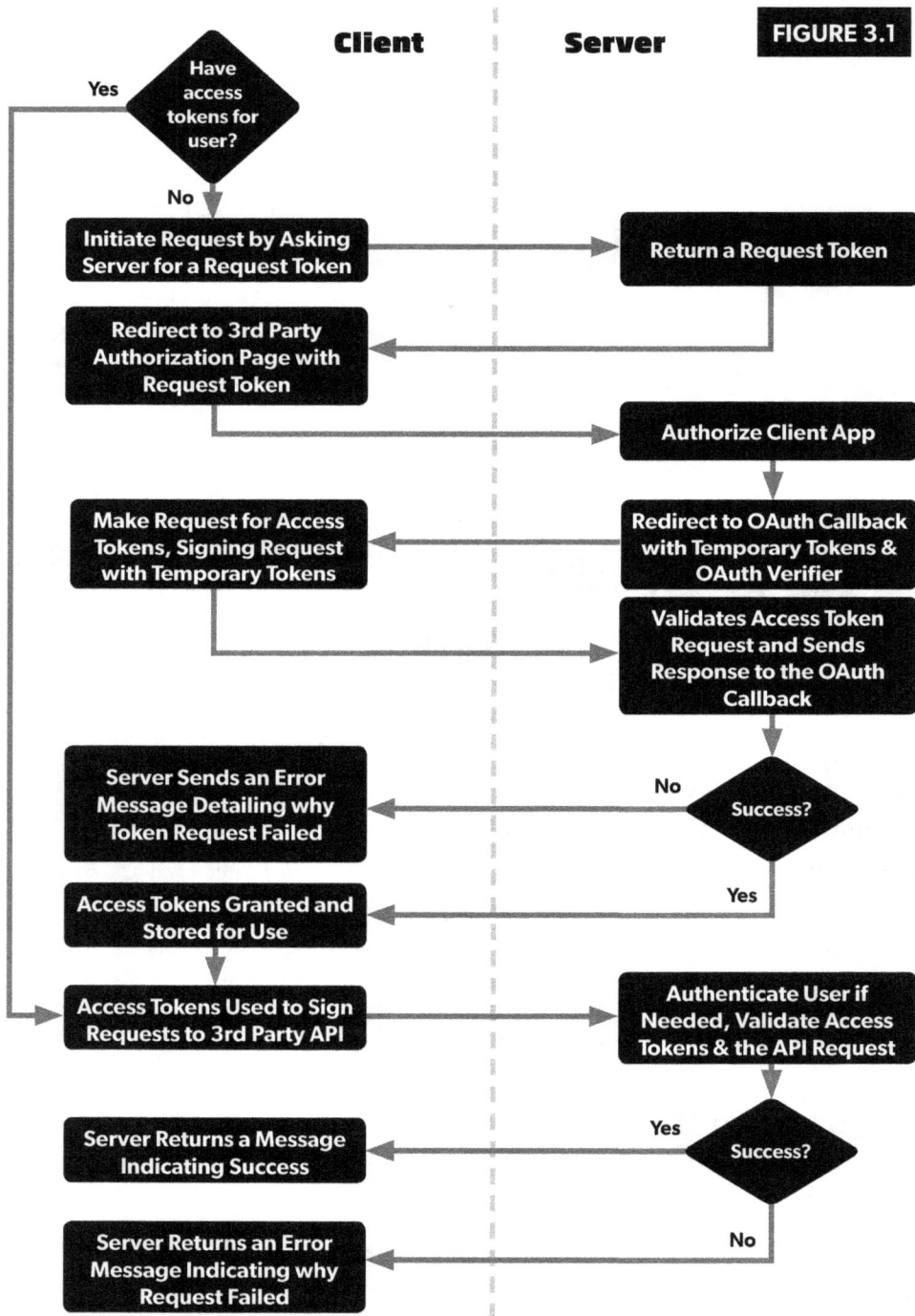

FIGURE 3.1

The header we're going to be paying particular attention to is the Authorization header. This header must be constructed correctly for an OAuth Server to be able to work with our requests. The Authorization header contains all the pertinent information needed to identify ourselves to the third-party service our client is trying to access. The Authorization header has a number of different components we will look at in detail. Knowing these will help you understand how to generate and use the components to create a valid OAuth request.

Let's get started by taking a look at the components of the Authorize header needed to create an OAuth Request. We'll start at the simple items and then move on to the more complex ones.

Version

Version is quite simply the version of OAuth you are trying to make a request against. Keep in mind the server you're trying to access will determine what value you should use here. Most services will tell you in the documentation what version of OAuth is supported. From that point on, it's up to you to set the version item in the header to the same version the server expects.

Timestamp

The timestamp is another pretty straight-forward value; it's the time you are making the request. In other words, most likely "right now". The value of timestamp is accepted as the number of seconds since the Unix epoch, so you don't have to do any sort of date formatting. In PHP, the time() function will give you the number of seconds since the Unix epoch. It can be safely utilized to create the timestamp you will use for the request.

Callback

If your request is supposed to do something after the request is made, you can provide a callback. A callback is the URL you expect to be directed to once the request is completed. The most common example is authenticating against a third party service. Once the authentication process happens, tokens are exchanged by redirecting you to the callback. From there, the tokens can be retrieved and stored or cached so other requests can be made with those tokens.

Signature Method

When you are ready to sign your request, you need to tell the OAuth Server how you signed it by specifying the Signature Method. There are three different options: HMAC-SHA1, RSA-SHA1, and Plaintext. This tells the server how it should attempt to parse and verify the signature. The use of Plaintext is generally not recommended, since no attempt is made to protect the information from man-in-the-middle attacks. If you must use Plaintext, it should **only** be used over TLS or SSL as they will encrypt the contents of the signature.

Token

The token is a value you retrieve from the third-party service you are using and it is used to identify you. When you authenticate to a service with your username and password, the service hands out tokens identifying you in future calls. Unlike username and password combinations, these tokens are created in a way to change somewhat regularly. The token in the Authorization header is used to identify you, but it is not the token secret or a combination of the 2 keys.

Consumer Key

The consumer key is a value identifying what application on the third party you are trying to access, and is also handed out by the server. Services provide the ability for a developer to determine the resources API users can access and the level of access they have to those resources. To execute this, many services require you to create or register an API application through their developer portal. The registered application identifies whether the API should be use for read or read/write access, and in some cases, which resources are accessible through the API. Upon creation of this application, the server responds with a key & secret pair known as the Consumer Key and Consumer Secret. The consumer key is sent in the Authorization header and identifies the application, ensuring the server can issue responses in accordance with the settings of the API application.

Nonce

A nonce is a string that will not be used more than once in a reasonable amount of time. It's used as a protection against replay attacks. Any request made with a nonce which has been used recently will be rejected by the server. This prevents attackers from reissuing the same request. Since the nonce is part of the signature, the signature must be regenerated with a new nonce to correctly re-sign a new request.

Signature

The signature is where all these important pieces of information are combined and encrypted. It allows the server to determine who you are and protects your credentials from being read in plain-text. Later in the chapter we'll see the process for generating this signature in OAuth 1.0. For now, a simple overview will suffice.

Understanding Tokens

In the last section I introduced the concept of tokens, in this section we are going to explore them in depth. Tokens are used to identify a user or application to the OAuth server. Using tokens to identify a user eliminates the need to provide a username and password in the API call.

The tokens come in pairs, one part being a public token and the other a secret token. As the name implies, the secret token is to be kept a secret and is not transmitted with OAuth requests. Since both tokens are required to properly identify a user and the public access token is more easily discovered, it's very important to protect the secret key and store it securely.

Securing tokens can be achieved with a couple simple practices. The first practice is to avoid committing the values of the key, token, and secrets to your version control system. Even if you are using a private repository, there is no way of knowing whether the repository will remain private, so it's best practice to avoid committing the values. The second practice is avoid storing any files with these values in a publicly accessible location. If the values can be accessed through a web browser or through local storage in a browser, an attacker may be able to find these values and make requests on your behalf. Lastly, while you have to send the access token and consumer key in the Authorization header, it's important to never send the secret values in plain-text via an HTTP Request. Later in this chapter we'll be covering the composite key and its role in protecting the secret values from being sent in plain-text. I have found phpdotenv[1] to be a great method of storing these values.

Tokens are provided by the third party service when a user authenticates and grants permission for the application to access their information. The service will essentially "connect" the local user account to the tokens. Since we have the ability to grant access to the API application, we also have the ability to revoke access. The application is identified by a different public/secret token combination which allows you to manage what applications have access to your account on the third party service. This is also the mechanism which allows for the revocation of applications.

The other important concept to understand with tokens is they are designed to have a relatively short life. Tokens are regenerated with each authentication call, so if the tokens aren't maintained by the application using them, they will be new for each session. It is generally a good idea to take advantage of this characteristic, as it provides an additional layer of security for your account. Think of it as changing your password before every single login–that's essentially what is happening and it makes it more difficult for attackers to fixate on an account. While there are still the same concerns with the account on the third party service, it helps prevent your information from being compromised by another application or API. It is very important to use strong passwords and utilize secure practices for storing your credentials regardless of how they are being used.

Understanding the Signature

The most difficult aspect of making an OAuth request is signing the request. If this step is done incorrectly, it will cause any HTTP request sent to the API to be rejected with a 401/Unauthorized status. Another confusing aspect is certain services require the components of the Authorization header to be in alphabetical order (Twitter, for example) while other services don't require any particular order. This can be especially confusing when trying to make a request for the first time. Ideally, you should understand exactly what the OAuth server is expecting to receive, but it's usually safe to alphabetize the components by default. That way, your client generates requests any service will accept.

There are a few sub-components of the signature we'll want to define because they are vital to properly signing the requests. Understanding how these are generated will provide a better understanding of how all tokens and components of the Authorization header are used.

Base String

The Base String is a key component to building the signature. It contains different pieces of information delimited by the & character. Let's take a look at how this component of the signature should be generated.

---

[1]   https://github.com/vlucas/phpdotenv

HTTP Verb

The first piece of this component is the HTTP verb being used for the specific request. Of the HTTP verbs introduced in Chapter 1, the verbs we're most concerned with are DELETE, GET, POST, and PUT. Since every service is different, it's important to understand what verb is expected for each endpoint. The other important thing to remember is the verb should always be in all capital letters. For example, if you are making a GET request, the first piece of this component should be GET and not Get or get.

Resource URL

The second component of the base string is the resource URL, which is simply the endpoint you are trying to access. This should be URL encoded as well so all the special characters in the URL are identified by their ASCII code. It's recommended to use rawurlencode to encode this value. There isn't much else to this piece, other than to note it should be delimited by an ampersand.

Authorization Header Components

Finally, we need to append all the information from the Authorization header to this string, separating each key/value pair by an ampersand. These should also be URL encoded and while the specification states they should be in alphabetical order, some services don't actually require this. To avoid confusion, it's a good practice to always sort them alphabetically. Let's take a look at how we'd do this with a practical example, see Listing 3.1.

Listing 3.1

```
01. <?php
02. // values for all the headers
03. $authorization_header_values = [
04.     'oauth_nonce' => $nonce,
05.     'oauth_callback' => $callback,
06.     'oauth_signature_method' => 'HMAC-SHA1',
07.     'oauth_timestamp' => time(),
08.     'oauth_consumer_key' => $consumer_key,
09.     'oauth_token' => $token,
10.     'oauth_version' => '1.0'
11. ];
12.
13. // if there is no callback, don't send it
14. if (!isset($callback) || $callback === '') {
15.     unset($authorization_header_values['oauth_callback']);
16. }
17.
18. // build the base string and sort the
19. // authorization header values alphabetically by key
20. $temp_array = array();
21. ksort($authorization_header_values);
```

```
22. foreach ($authorization_header_values as $key => $value) {
23.     $temp_array[] = $key . '=' . rawurlencode($value);
24. }
25.
26. // unpack the values that we stored in the temporary array
27. $parameters = rawurlencode(implode('&', $temp_array));
```

As you can see, we build these last components similar to how a URL query string is constructed. Each key/value pair is denoted key=pair and each pair is delimited by an ampersand. You can also see by using ksort we're able to alphabetize these components by key name.

Looping through the parameters as we did in Listing 3.1 provides an explicit look at what happens with each parameter. It is possible to use http_build_query to generate the base string, Listing 3.2 is an example of how to do it with the proper encoding. Keep in mind, there are differences in how each service implements the base string so one script may not cover all use cases.

Listing 3.2

```
01. <?php
02. // values for all the headers
03. $authorization_header_values = [
04.     'oauth_nonce' => $nonce,
05.     'oauth_callback' => $callback,
06.     'oauth_signature_method' => 'HMAC-SHA1',
07.     'oauth_timestamp' => time(),
08.     'oauth_consumer_key' => $consumer_key,
09.     'oauth_token' => $token,
10.     'oauth_version' => '1.0'
11. ];
12.
13. // if there is no callback, don't send it
14. if ($callback === '') {
15.     unset($authorization_header_values['oauth_callback']);
16. }
17.
18. // build the base string
19. $temp_array = array();
20. ksort($authorization_header_values);
21.
22. $parameters = rawurlencode(http_build_query($authorization_header_values));
```

Putting It All Together

So by using the example in Listing 3.1 and combining the results from the script with other components, we can build the base string. Let's assume we're making a GET request to https://example.org/user/bce123df4a, which will be stored in the variable $endpoint, and the output from the script in the listing is assigned to a variable $parameters. To build the base string we'd simply concatenate the values like so.

```
$base_string = 'GET&' . rawurlencode($endpoint) . '&' . $parameters;
```

It's important to note, since we URL encoded the parameters in the script, we don't need to do it again here. Now we have the first component of our signature constructed and can move on to the next step.

This section will conclude with an example of a complete base string which was generated for a Twitter API request. (Note all keys and tokens in this request are not active and cannot be used to make a request).

```
GET&https%3A%2F%2Fapi.twitter.com%2F1.1%2Fstatuses%2Fuser_timeline.json&count
%3D2%26oauth_consumer_key%3DRuk5McRjIKd2DP22n3afjw%26oauthnonce%3Dd303ed
ff00aaaad160688d8acab54bc6%26oauth_signature_method%3DHMAC-SHA1%26oauth_
timestamp%3D1445350048%26oauth_token%3D162aaaaa-yZJSlFednBab8zFJDZvSQ9AEDicAW2aHKcaH
iBUaJ%26oauth_version%3D1.0%26screen_name%3Dtwitterapi
```

The output above has been wrapped for display in this book. In reality, it's a single, continuous string.

Composite Key

The Composite Key makes use of the secret keys assigned to the user (Consumer Secret) and the application (access secret). This step is more straight-forward and quite simply the Composite Key is hashed with the base string according to our signature method.

Simply put, to generate the composite key all we need to do is URL encode each key separately and delimit them with an ampersand. The Consumer Secret is first and the access secret comes next. Let's assume our Consumer Secret is stored in $consumer_secret and the Access secret is stored in $access_secret. We end up with an implementation which looks something like this:

```
$composite_key = rawurlencode($consumer_secret) . '&'
                . rawurlencode($access_secret);
```

Hashing the Signature

Now that we have a properly generated base string and composite key, the final step in the process is to hash them according to the signature method we've provided. It's important the method we specify and the manner in which we hash the values are the same. We're essentially telling the OAuth server how we created the signature so it knows how to validate our request. To demonstrate this quickly, we'll assume the base string is stored in $base_string and the composite key is stored in $composite_key. If we specified SHA1, our hashing implementation will look like:

```
$signature = base64_encode( hash_hmac('sha1', $base_string, $composite_key, true) );
```

As you might have noticed from Listing 3.1, we don't have a component for the signature. Now that we have a signature, it should be pretty easy to set it in the Authorization header. We just need to make sure we create a key called oauth_signature and assign the value of the key to the value of $signature we just generated. Once it is added to the Authorization header, the request can be sent and should validate properly by the OAuth server.

Understanding the Nonce

We have familiarized ourselves with tokens and understand how to build the OAuth signature, but there still might be a word that looks unfamiliar. What exactly is a *nonce*? According to Webster's Dictionary it is "a word or expression coined for or used on one occasion". In the programming world, we'd call it a string and the rest of the definition fits the bill. It's a string which is passed along with the request and is only used once. This means that every single request you send has a unique, unpredictable nonce.

In practice, this is a randomly generated hash and it's used to protect from replay attacks. So while the word looks funny, there's really not much to it. All you really need to remember is you shouldn't use the same nonce value more than once.

To generate a nonce we need to generate a random string of characters and then hash them. There are some different techniques for doing this, below is one example.

```
$bytes = openssl_random_pseudo_bytes(16);
$string = bin2hex($bytes);
$nonce = hash(sha512, $string);
var_dump($nonce);
```

Will produce a nonce like:

```
string(128) "9e23987cf0da2f907d0eda3779bd5d4539a40d7904338c8f198ec4a37f62a4154
44653e6a443aeb4f271c1f892d8b6fe0d2246fbfe778e5359c6b9626b6b71c2"
```

Forming a Valid OAuth 1.0 Request

We've dissected the components of an OAuth 1.0 request and should have a little bit more simplified view of how these requests are made. By taking the individual components apart, what once seemed really complex now seems a bit more realistic to grasp. How do we tie this all together? The following example is going to be an implementation of a class building an OAuth 1.0 request. For clarity's sake, I'm going to comment the code in a way which explains what I'm doing. This example is going to be a call to a fake API with made-up tokens. Without further delay, let's look at our classes.

Listing 3.3 shows a basic class for holding our consumer information. This will hold the token and secret generated when we register our application with an external service.

Listing 3.3
```php
01. <?php
02. /**
03.  * Class to hold our Consumer information
04.  */
05. class OAuthConsumer
06. {
07.     /**
08.      * Consumer token
09.      * @var string $token
10.      */
11.     public $token;
12.
13.     /**
14.      * Consumer secret
15.      * @var string $secret
16.      */
17.     public $secret;
18. }
```

We also need a class to store access information returned when a user grants us access.

Listing 3.4
```php
19. <?php
20. /**
21.  * Class to hold our access information
22.  */
23. class OAuthAccess
24. {
25.     /**
26.      * Access Token
27.      * @var string $token
28.      */
29.     public $token;
30.
31.     /**
32.      * Access Secret
33.      * @var string $secret
34.      */
35.     public $secret;
36. }
```

Next, the OAuthHeader class in Listing 3.5 does the hard work of building our Base String, Authorization header, and the signature for our request.

Listing 3.5

```php
01. <?php
02. /**
03.  * Class to build our OAuth Headers
04.  */
05. class OAuthHeader
06. {
07.     /**
08.      * Callback value, if any
09.      * @var string $callback
10.      */
11.     protected $callback = '';
12.
13.     /**
14.      * Value for the nonce
15.      * @var string $nonce
16.      */
17.     protected $nonce;
18.
19.     /**
20.      * Request URL
21.      * @var string $request_url
22.      */
23.     protected $request_url;
24.
25.     /**
26.      * HTTP Verb
27.      * @var string $http_verb
28.      */
29.     protected $http_verb;
30.
31.     /**
32.      * Consumer Object
33.      * @var OAuthConsumer $consumer
34.      */
35.     protected $consumer;
36.
37.     /**
38.      * Access Object
39.      * @var OAuthAccess $access
40.      */
41.     protected $access;
42.
```

```php
43.    /**
44.     * Constructor for OAuthHeader
45.     * @param OAuthConsumer $consumer
46.     * @param OAuthAccess $access
47.     */
48.    public function __construct(OAuthConsumer $consumer, OAuthAccess $access) {
49.        $this->consumer = $consumer;
50.        $this->access = $access;
51.    }
52.
53.    /**
54.     * Accessor method to set the nonce
55.     * @param string $nonce
56.     */
57.    public function setNonce($nonce) {
58.        $this->nonce = $nonce;
59.    }
60.
61.    /**
62.     * Accessor method to get the nonce
63.     * @return string
64.     */
65.    public function getNonce() {
66.        return $this->nonce;
67.    }
68.
69.    /**
70.     * Accessor method to set the verb
71.     * @param string $verb
72.     */
73.    public function setHTTPVerb($verb) {
74.        $this->http_verb = $verb;
75.    }
76.
77.    /**
78.     * Accessor method to get the verb
79.     * @return string
80.     */
81.    public function getVerb() {
82.        return $this->http_verb;
83.    }
84.
85.    /**
86.     * Accessor method to set request url
87.     * @param string $request_url
88.     */
89.    public function setRequestURL($request_url) {
90.        $this->request_url = $request_url;
91.    }
```

```
92.
93.     /**
94.      * Accessor method to get request url
95.      * @return string
96.      */
97.     public function getRequestURL() {
98.         return $this->request_url;
99.     }
100.
101.    /**
102.     * Accessor method to set the callback
103.     * @param string $callback
104.     */
105.    public function setCallback($callback) {
106.        $this->callback = $callback;
107.    }
108.
109.    /**
110.     * Accessor method to get the callback
111.     * @return string
112.     */
113.    public function getCallback() {
114.        return $this->callback;
115.    }
116.
117.    /**
118.     * Method to organize the values that will make up
119.     * the authorize header
120.     * @return array
121.     */
122.    protected function setHeaderInfo() {
123.        $authorize_params = [
124.            'oauth_nonce' => $this->getNonce(),
125.            'oauth_callback' => $this->getCallback(),
126.            'oauth_signature_method' => 'HMAC-SHA1',
127.            'oauth_timestamp' => time(),
128.            'oauth_consumer_key' => $this->consumer->token,
129.            'oauth_token' => $this->access->token,
130.            'oauth_version' => '1.0'
131.        ];
132.
133.        if ($this->callback == '') {
134.            unset($authorize_params['oauth_callback']);
135.        }
136.        return $authorize_params;
137.    }
138.
```

```php
139.    /**
140.     * Method to buid the base string for the signature
141.     * @param array $authorize_params
142.     * @return string
143.     */
144.    protected function buildBaseString($params) {
145.        $temp_array = array();
146.        ksort($params);
147.        foreach ($params as $key => $value) {
148.            $temp_array[] = $key . '=' . rawurlencode($value);
149.        }
150.
151.        return $this->http_verb . '&' . rawurlencode($this->request_url) . '&'
152.                . rawurlencode(implode('&', $temp_array));
153.    }
154.
155.    /**
156.     * Method to build the composite key for the signature
157.     * @return string
158.     */
159.    protected function buildCompositeKey() {
160.        return rawurlencode($this->consumer->secret) . '&'
161.                . rawurlencode($this->access->secret);
162.    }
163.
164.    /**
165.     * Method to construct the authorization header
166.     * @param array $params
167.     * @return string
168.     */
169.    protected function buildAuthHeader($params) {
170.        $header_prefix = 'Authorization: OAuth ';
171.        $values = array();
172.        foreach ($params as $key => $value) {
173.            $values[] = $key . '=' . rawurlencode($value);
174.        }
175.        $header_contents = implode(',', $values);
176.        return $header_prefix . $header_contents;
177.    }
178.
```

```
179.    /**
180.     * Method to build the signature
181.     * @param string $base_string
182.     * @param string $composite_key
183.     * @return string
184.     */
185.    protected function buildSignature($base_string, $composite_key) {
186.        return base64_encode(hash_hmac('sha1', $base_string, $composite_key, true));
187.    }
188.
189.    /**
190.     * Method to return the entire OAuth Request header
191.     * ready to use
192.     * @return string
193.     */
194.    public function getAuthorizationHeader()    {
195.        $params = $this->setHeaderInfo();
196.        $base_string = $this->buildBaseString($params);
197.        $composite_key = $this->buildCompositeKey();
198.        $sig = $this->buildSignature($base_string, $composite_key);
199.        $params['oauth_signature'] = $sig;
200.        return $this->buildAuthHeader($params);
201.    }
202. }
```

So there we've knocked a pretty straight-forward implementation which will generate the full authorization header for us. Is this perfect? Probably not, but as you can see the intent was to demystify the process of making an OAuth request yourself. As I stated earlier on, it's always a great idea to use something tried and true. I mean, if it works correctly, there's no sense in reinventing it, right?

This chapter explained the details of what's actually happening when an OAuth request is made. If for some reason the need exists to recreate an OAuth request class, you now understand how this process flows. This wouldn't be complete without an example of how to execute this code, so let's take a look at Listing 3.6 to see how to execute this and what the resulting output looks like.

Listing 3.6

```
01. <?php
02. include_once __DIR__ . '/listing.3.3.php';
03. include_once __DIR__ . '/listing.3.4.php';
04. include_once __DIR__ . '/listing.3.5.php';
05.
06. $consumer = new OAuthConsumer();
07. $consumer->token = 'ab234efdce1294855';
08. $consumer->secret = 'b77462342fdedfeaefe23423434310098';
09.
```

```
10.  $access = new OAuthAccess();
11.  $access->token = '1efe342faade88421';
12.  $access->secret = 'ccfedb764234094234212defe';
13.
14.  $headers = new OAuthHeader($consumer, $access);
15.  /**
16.   * There would generally be a method that generates this for you or
17.   * building the headers would
18.   * generate a new nonce, doing it this for simplicity.
19.   */
20.  $headers->setNonce('bfefacdede123213');
21.  $headers->setHTTPVerb('GET');
22.  $headers->setRequestURL('https://api.example.com/v1/user/bcdef12345');
23.  $header = $headers->getAuthorizationHeader();
24.  print $header;
```

You can see this listing provides a relatively straight-forward interface for using this class. What happens when you run it? You should get output similar to the following (as a single string):

```
Authorization: OAuth oauth_nonce=bfefacdede123213,
oauth_signature_method=HMAC-SHA1, oauth_timestamp=1389156921,
oauth_consumer_key=ab234efdce1294856,
oauth_token=1efe342faade88421, oauth_version=1.0,
oauth_signature=3Ey74KvTkPjyVqodd3GtLX%2BlHPs%3D
```

You see a full OAuth Authorization header ready for you to use!

Chapter
4

OAuth 1 Server

Once you find you need to provide content or services from your application to external applications, it's important you are able to accurately identify the users making a request to your service. This is where the OAuth server comes into play. If you can't identify and authorize actions properly, you will not be able to offer a service people will actually use. Protecting your users' content and account information is the foundation to building a secure application. Let's take a look at how this flow works.

The OAuth 1 Client chapter focused on how to build the authorization headers required to make a valid OAuth request. It's important to note, if we aren't implementing our own service, we don't ever have to worry about the implementation of an OAuth server. However, once we know we are going to receive and process OAuth requests, it's important we understand how to analyze them correctly.

Analyzing Request Components

If you haven't read the previous chapter on building the OAuth 1 request and don't have a strong understanding about what is actually sent in an OAuth request, now would be a good time to brush up. When analyzing the requests we receive, it's important to understand how they are built. You should read the previous chapter before we proceed.

The information we will see in the request is contained in the Authorization header. We will need to be able to retrieve and parse the information in this header in order to verify the request and authorization attempt. Once we are able to retrieve the header and parse it into the individual components, we can build the signature we expect the request to be signed with. Since we issued the tokens, our Oauth server can retrieve the consumer secret for the consumer key which was sent, build the signature it expects, and compare that signature to the signature sent by the Oauth client. Since we have all the information needed to build the base string and can retrieve the information for the composite key from our own data stores, validating a signed request is straightforward.

Getting the Authorization Header

The first step to analyze any Oauth request we receive obviously requires us to obtain the information in the Authorization header. PHP stores many of the request headers in the `$_SERVER` superglobal; if you wanted to access the value of the `Accept` header, all you would have to do is refer to `$_SERVER['HTTP_ACCEPT']`. Pretty easy right? If you read through the PHP documentation on server variables[1], you'll notice in the `$_SERVER` superglobal section there is no mention of the `Authorization` header.

Since we can't use `$_SERVER`, we have a few options for retrieving the `Authorization` value. Depending on your needs, both are good options. The first option is to use the `apache_response_headers()` function. As you might suspect, this will return an associative array of all the Apache response headers in the current request. This is the more programmatic way to do it, it doesn't require any sort of configuration. It also makes it pretty easy to use what you need and ignore anything you don't need.

The second option requires the use of Apache `mod_rewrite`, which can map the values of a specific header to the `$_SERVER` superglobal. By adding this rewrite rule to your `.htaccess` or host configuration file, you'll be able to add the additional headers you'd like to use to the `$_SERVER` superglobal. The rule for the Authorization header looks like this:

```
RewriteEngine on
RewriteRule .* - [E=HTTP_AUTHORIZATION:%{HTTP:Authorization}]
```

For all requests, this rewrite rule sets an environment variable called `HTTP_AUTHORIZATION` to the value of the HTTP header, `Authorization`. The prerequisite to this approach is having `mod_rewrite` installed and having the ability to override with an `.htaccess` file.

If you are using `nginx` instead of `Apache`, you can use the `getallheaders()` PHP function. This function will return an array of all the request headers, the Authorization header can be retrieved from this array. The PHP manual has more information about using `getallheaders()` [2] to retrieve Request Headers.

---

[1]   http://php.net/reserved.variables.server
[2]   http://php.net/function.getallheaders

Reading the Information in the Header

Once we have the information from the header extracted, we essentially have a large comma-delimited string of key value pairs. That's the information we want to work with, but to make it easier on ourselves, we'd probably rather have an associative array to work with. Let's look at an example of how we easily break this out in Listing 4.1.

Listing 4.1

```php
01. <?php
02. $header_value = <<<EOH
03. oauth_nonce="1acef0fefeafe4cae0", oauth_signature_method="HMAC-SHA1",
04. oauth_timestamp="1391036000", oauth_consumer_key="xxxxxxxxxxxxxxx",
05. oauth_token="xxxxxxxxxxxxxxxxxxxxxxxxxxxxxxxxxxxxxxxxxx",
06. oauth_version="1.0", oauth_signature="xxxxxxxxxxxxxxxxxxxxxxxxxxxxxxxxxxx"
07. EOH;
08.
09. $authorization = array();
10. foreach (explode(',', $header_value) as $pair) {
11.     list($key, $value) = explode('=', $pair);
12.     $authorization[$key] = trim($value);
13. }
14.
15. var_dump($authorization);
```

Once you have the information broken out this way, it becomes much easier to use it to verify the request coming in, see below.

```
array(7) {
  'oauth_nonce' =>
  string(20) ""1acef0fefeafe4cae0""
  'oauth_signature_method' =>
  string(11) ""HMAC-SHA1""

oauth_timestamp' =>
  string(12) ""1391036000""
  'oauth_consumer_key' =>
  string(18) ""xxxxxxxxxxxxxxx""

oauth_token' =>
  string(42) ""xxxxxxxxxxxxxxxxxxxxxxxxxxxxxxxxxxxxxxxxxx""

oauth_version' =>
  string(5) ""1.0""
  'oauth_signature' =>
  string(35) ""xxxxxxxxxxxxxxxxxxxxxxxxxxxxxxxxxxx""
}
```

Finally

At this point, you'll be able to do some very basic checks on the request data. For instance, if you are expecting an OAuth 1.0 request and it comes in as an OAuth 2.0 request, you'll be able to deal with it prior to even validating the signature. You also could do a check on the oauth_timestamp to make sure it's relatively recent before trying to proceed. We're going to need a few other things in order to build the signature we'll need to compare, but we'll take a look at it in the next section.

Verifying Signatures

So we have the request and all the individual components from the Authorization header, there are a few other things we need to collect before we can start building the signature. We know from the last chapter the signature is comprised of the composite key and the base string. All that is essentially left for us to do is create the signature we're expecting and compare it to what was sent by the client.

Composite Key

The composite key is made up of consumer secret and the access secret. You might have noticed those values aren't coming over anywhere in the request, at least not in a way we can use them. The server distributed these keys to the client when the user granted access, which means the server should still be storing these keys. The server will retrieve the secrets keys from the storage engine where they are stored. The client will provide the public key and token. With this information in hand, the server has everything needed to build the expected composite key. Building the composite key is as simple as:

```
$keys = array();
// order is important consumer key always comes first
$keys['consumer_secret'] = rawurlencode($consumer_secret);
$keys['access_secret'] = rawurlencode($access_secret);

$composite_key = implode('&', $keys);
```

As long as we ensure we use rawurlencode on both values and lead with the consumer secret, creating the composite key is a simple thing to do.

Base String

The base string is a bit more involved, we have more values to combine and a few more things we need to collect before we can build this. As we discussed in earlier chapters, HTTP verbs are very important to understand. We need to make sure we act accordingly when a request is sent, sending a GET request to a resource expecting a POST request shouldn't create a resource. The first value in the base string is the HTTP verb, this helps us confirm the request is being sent the with the correct action. We can retrieve that with $_SERVER['REQUEST_METHOD'].

The next piece of information we need is the URL to the resource we are requesting. This part of the signature ensures the request and what we're trying to process are the same endpoint or resource. This can be easily built from $_SERVER values as well:

```
$url = 'https://' . $_SERVER['HTTP_HOST'] . $_SERVER['REQUEST_URI']
```

The first two pieces of the base string have been found. Now we're going to need some logic to create the final component of the base string.

Remember all those values we extracted in the previous session and how deftly we stored them in an associative array? It's time to get ready to use those again. If you remember, we had to alphabetize the OAuth values in order to build the request, so we're going to do it again. In the previous example, our array was stored in a variable called $authorization. In order to sort and build the string, we need to do the following:

```
ksort($authorization);
$temp_array = array();
// unset the signature, since we're building it
unset($authorization['oauth_signature']);
foreach ($authorization as $key => $value) {
    $temp_array[] = $key . '=' . $value;
}
$params = rawurlencode(implode('&', $temp_array));
```

This code sorts the array alphabetically by key and stores the key and value pair as a string in a temporary array. Once the array is populated with all the key value pairs, we create a string which has each set of values delimited by the ampersand character. After we rawurlencode the string, we almost have our base string complete. The only remaining thing to do is to take our verb and URL, rawurlencode them individually and prefix them to the string with ampersand delimiters. It may sound confusing, but let's see the code; it's not complicated.

```
$verb = $_SERVER['REQUEST_METHOD'];
// $params is used from the last example and already encoded
$base_string = rawurlencode($verb) . rawurlencode($url) . $params;
```

That's it! We have our base string and we're ready to build the signature.

Building the Signature

The complicated part is essentially over, with these two values we can hash and compare. The most important aspect of actually constructing the signature is using the same hashing method the request used. We're able to figure it out by looking at the oauth_signature_method value in the Authorization header. Generally, we're looking for either HMAC-SHA1, RSA-SHA1 or PLAINTEXT, this is going to determine how we hash the signature. Since HMAC-SHA1 is commonly used, we can see the signature is hashed and base64_encoded.

```
$signature = base64_encode(
    hash_hmac('sha1',$base_string, $composite, true)
);
```

That's it, we have our signature! From this point forward, all we need to do is pull the `oauth_signature` value from our `$authorization` array and compare it to the signature we just built. If the expected and submitted signatures match, the user has been identified correctly and moves on to the next step in the process.

Distributing Tokens

Now that we know how to reproduce and verify the inbound signature, it's important to understand the server is the entity responsible for generating and distributing the necessary tokens. Tokens provide a way for us to identify users and applications without requiring them to provide easily identifiable information (user names, application names, etc.).

The tokens can be regenerated at the user's request, so it's important to generate the tokens in an easily repeatable way. It's also important they are complex enough to be reasonably resistant to attempts to guess them or brute force attack them, especially the secret tokens.

Tokens are generally distributed by making a call to an authorization endpoint, in which the 3rd party application will authenticate the user name and password and redirect them to an endpoint on your page with the tokens. This process will then associate the tokens to the authenticated user so they can be identified by the tokens. The tokens are generally hashes and should not contain any human readable information.

Handling Authentication Failures

What happens if the signatures don't match? Obviously, for the protection of our data and the security of our application we cannot allow requests with mismatched signatures to proceed any further. We have to communicate back to the requesting party their request was not executed successfully. Generally, we communicate this information with the use of HTTP status codes, discussed in Chapter 1.

HTTP status codes allow us to tell the user what went wrong, without divulging too much information. Specific error messages often reveal more about the request than is necessary, which gives very vital information to anyone seeking to obtain access fraudulently. In the case of a mismatched signature, we simply need to inform the requesting agent that, "based on the information you sent over, you are not authorized to perform the action you requested on the resource in your request". This, of course, would be the 401 status code and would communicate exactly what we need to respond with, no more and no less. You can use the `header` function for this.

```
header('HTTP/1.0 401 Unauthorized');
```

To relate this back to the familiar domain of web pages and login screens, a mismatched signature is simply a bad login attempt. When we manage logins with our authentication system, we typically store the secret part of the credentials (the password) by using the password hashing API to generate a unique one-way hash. When the user submits their user name and password through our login form, a hash is generated for the submitted password and compared to the one we stored earlier. So you see, we are already familiar with a less involved "signature creation process". If the password isn't encrypted with the same algorithm and salt, it won't match and we won't be able to authenticate the user. Though I will readily admit, the OAuth process for creating these signatures is a lot more involved than hashing a password.

Handling Authorization Failures

We also run into situations where we can identify the user, but the user is asking to do something they are not permitted to do, such as posting a status on someone else's behalf. The tricky part of authorization is every service has different requirements and expectations on what users are allowed to access.

> Remember, OAuth helps you to mange Authenticating users so you can be certain they are who they say they are. It does not take care of checking if they are authorized to do what they are asking to do.

Generally speaking, taking "destructive" actions are restricted to the owner or group of owners of the resource. Destructive actions would be the creation, alteration, or removal of a resource. Authorization is ultimately a step that will need to be handled by yourself. Your service is free to grant access to resources based on the rules of your business or domain, OAuth will not restrict that in any way. Essentially, a properly signed request is saying, "Hello, I'm Matt, here's my ID and yes I'm happy to wait for you to run it through your system". If the other part of my request is, "I'd like to post a hilarious tweet on Sally's account," the service has to determine if it is acceptable for Matt to do and then allow or deny the action.

Generally speaking, the status codes which are used to communicate back to the requesting party are `401/Unauthorized` or `403/Forbidden`. In both status codes, the understanding is that the request was received and understood, but lacked the appropriate authorization for the requested resource. Using a `403/Forbidden` response, communicates Authorization will not help and the request should not be repeated. This is another great example of how using the HTTP status codes we presented in <u>Chapter 1</u> clearly communicate the result of the request. As a matter of best practice and consistency, every request should return the appropriate HTTP status code in favor of creating a "custom" response code.

Summary

We looked at how an OAuth 1 Server processes a request and learned the OAuth signature is an effective way of verifying the identity of a user. We should also understand why it is important to protect our access secret and consumer secret. This chapter provided insight on how to start implementing an OAuth 1 server and gave you a glimpse into some of the specific security matters you'll need to keep in mind.

OAuth 1 Server

Chapter
5

OAuth 1 Implementation

We've covered OAuth 1 in detail; you have a general idea of why it exists and how it works. Now it's time to look at using OAuth 1 in a more practical sense. If you skipped to this chapter and don't have a decent grasp on the basics of HTTP or a basic of understanding of what OAuth 1 was created to do, I would encourage you to read the previous chapters. This chapter includes a signficant amount of example code. I encourage you to have a clear understanding of any code you didn't write before implementing it in your own project.

This chapter will cover implementations in a couple of different categories. We're going to take a look at existing OAuth 1 libraries and how to use them. We will also investigate two framework implementations, namely Zend Framework and Symfony. We will finish with example exercises where we will actually create some calls to well-known OAuth 1 Service Providers. The code here is going to be more than theoretical, it has been tested to work with all these frameworks and services as of the time of this writing.

Existing Libraries

One of the largest problems we come across in the software development industry is the amount of work it takes to verify whether an existing collection of code is trustworthy enough for us to use. Frequently, we would rather put the work towards getting our project done, even if it means writing our own solution instead of using an existing one. The more quickly we can understand and verify the existing code will fulfill our needs in a secure manner, the more quickly we can implement it and move on to other aspects of our project or application. I present these existing libraries without opinion as components to consider if OAuth is going to be part of your next project.

OAuth PECL Extension

The PHP Extension Community Library (PECL) has an OAuth package which can be used to make OAuth 1 requests. Since it's an extension, it has to be installed, compiled, and the extension has to be enabled in your php.ini file before you can use it to make OAuth 1 requests.

Installing

Installing the PECL extension is pretty straight forward. You'll need to have the PHP source files, build tools (autoconf, automake, libtool, and more), and a compiler. For complete instructions, see the PECL installation docs[1]. Assuming you have everything needed to compile them, at the command line you can type:

```
pecl install oauth
```

An easier alternative, you should be able to install it via your Linux distribution's package repository. For OS X, see Rob Allen's post on setting up PHP & Mysql for specific instructions.[2] It's important to make sure you have permission to install extensions; you may have to run this command as sudo or have an admin install the OAuth extension for you.

Once you have the extension installed, you must enable the extension in your php.ini. The same permission requirements exist, so you'll either have to use sudo or have a server admin edit the file for you. Once you've located your php.ini (which you can do with php -i from the command line), all you need to do is add the line:

```
extension=oauth.so
```

If you are writing a command line script, it should start working. If you are running a script through a web server, restart your web server to enable the extension. You can check if it's installed with the function phpinfo(). You should see the output as in Fiugre 5.1.

FIGURE 5.1

OAuth	
OAuth support	enabled
PLAINTEXT support	enabled
RSA-SHA1 support	enabled
HMAC-SHA1 support	enabled
Request engine support	php_streams, curl
source version	$Id: oauth.c 325799 2012-05-24 21:07:51Z jawed $
version	1.2.3

[1]   http://php.net/install.pecl.intro
[2]   Setting up PHP & MySQL on OS X Mavericks: http://akrabat.com/phpmavericks

Code

In this section, we're actually going to review code. The first code example demonstrates how to retrieve consumer tokens. The other snippet of code uses the PECL extension to retrieve a tweet from the Twitter REST API. In addition to the code, there will be an explanation as to what the code is actually doing. It is important to note this code snippet won't utilize every available option, but it should give you a good idea of how to use the extension.

When you create and register an application on Twitter, for example, you are assigned an API key and a handful of URLs which will ensure a user gets authenticated correctly.

> NOTE: Head over to *https://apps.twitter.com* to register a Twitter app. Once you register, you will find your API key under **Application Settings**. Ensure that under the **Permissions** tab you ask for Read, Write, and Access Direct Messages access.

Since we're asking Twitter (in other examples it could be some other service) to handle the difficult part of ensuring a user is who they say they are, we have to be prepared to receive the response from the authentication request. The application itself has an API Key and an API Secret, which allows us to identify the context in which we are trying to use the API. A user has the same type of tokens, which will allow Twitter to identify them and make sure they are interacting with the API in a way allowed by the application. Let's take a look at how the PECL extension allows us to do this.

FIGURE 5.2

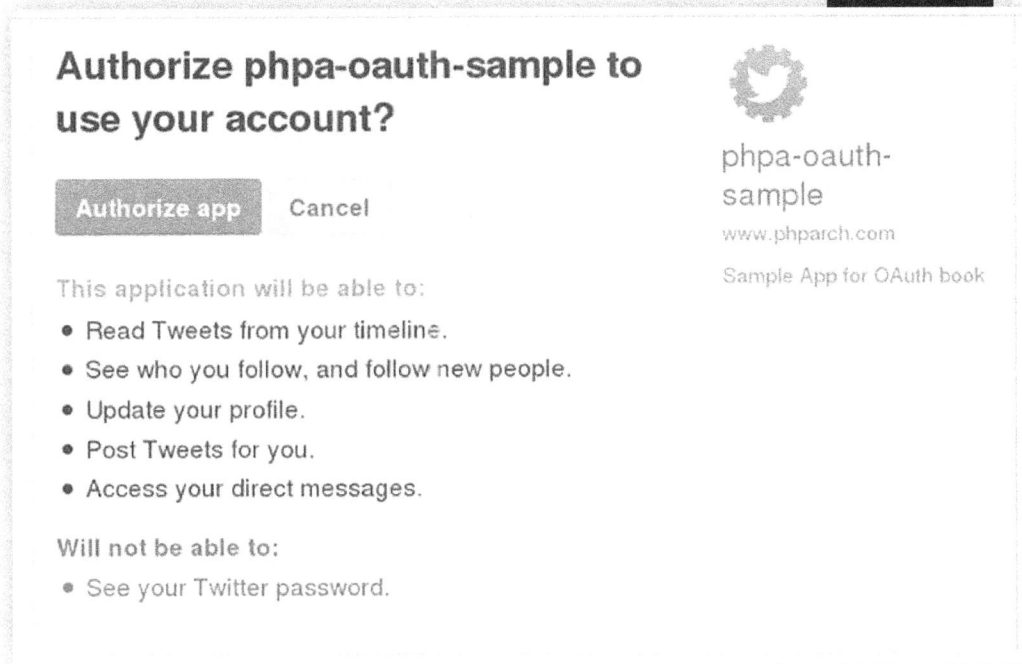

Authorize phpa-oauth-sample to use your account?

Authorize app   Cancel

This application will be able to:
- Read Tweets from your timeline.
- See who you follow, and follow new people.
- Update your profile.
- Post Tweets for you.
- Access your direct messages.

Will not be able to:
- See your Twitter password.

phpa-oauth-sample
www.phparch.com
Sample App for OAuth book

Use PHP's built in web server to try the code below. Save Listing 5.1 as `index.php` *and Listing 5.2 as* `callback.php` *in an empty directory. Then start it with* `php -S 127.0.0.1:8080` *while in that directory. For this to work, you'll have to set* `http://127.0.0.1:8080/callback.php` *in your Twitter application as the callback URL.*

Listing 5.1. index.php

```
01. <?php
02. /**
03.  * This code is going to show us how we retrieve OAuth tokens with the
04.  * PECL OAuth Extension
05.  */
06.
07. // API Key/Secret keys
08. $api_key = 'YOUR_APPLICATION_KEY';
09. $api_secret = 'YOUR_APPLICATION_SECRET';
10.
11. // the urls we'll need to authorize/authenticate
12. $base = 'https://api.twitter.com';
13. $request_url = $base . '/oauth/request_token';
14. $access_url = $base . '/oauth/access_token';
15. $authorize_url = $base . '/oauth/authorize';
16.
17. try {
18.     $oauth = new OAuth($api_key, $api_secret, OAUTH_SIG_METHOD_HMACSHA1,
19.                        OAUTH_AUTH_TYPE_URI);
20.     $oauth->enableDebug(); // turn this off in production...
21.
22.     // First we need to get our temporary OAuth
23.     // credentials (Request Tokens)
24.     $request_token = $oauth->getRequestToken($request_url);
25.
26.     // this will send info back that we can use to authorize
27.     header('Location: ' . $authorize_url . '?oauth_token='
28.            . $request_token['oauth_token']);
29. } catch (OAuthException $e) {
30.     print_r($e);
31. }
```

Listing 5.2. callback.php

```php
01. <?php
02. /**
03.  * Now that we've gone out to twitter and authorized, we'll be directed to the callback.
04.  * We can exchange those temporary credentials for access tokens.
05.  */
06.
07. // API Key/Secret keys
08. $api_key = 'YOUR_APPLICATION_KEY';
09. $api_secret = 'YOUR_APPLICATION_SECRET';
10.
11. // the urls we'll need to authorize/authenticate
12. $base = 'https://api.twitter.com';
13. $access_url = $base . '/oauth/access_token';
14.
15. try {
16.     $oauth = new OAuth($api_key, $api_secret, OAUTH_SIG_METHOD_HMACSHA1,
17.                        OAUTH_AUTH_TYPE_URI);
18.
19.     // we've been redirected to our callback, the OAuth token and verifier are in the
20.     // query string
21.     $oauth->setToken($_GET['oauth_token'], '');
22.
23.     // The second param is an authorization session handle, not all APIs use this. By
24.     // passing the verifier in as the 3rd parameter, you are verifying the request.
25.     $access_tokens = $oauth->getAccessToken($access_url, '', $_GET['oauth_verifier']);
26.
27.     // response will have screen_name, user_id, oauth_token, and oauth_token_secret.
28.     // You would need to persist these in some way.
29.     var_dump($access_tokens);
30. } catch(OAuthException $e) {
31.     print_r($e);
32. }
```

Once you have successfully requested temporary tokens and exchanged them for access tokens, you'll be able to use the returned tokens to make requests on behalf of the user. It's important to note while the access tokens in OAuth 1 tend to have a very long life, the request tokens do not. The request tokens may only last a minute or two, so it's important to this process for those exchanges to be as quickly as possible. If the tokens expire, the user will have to ask for new request tokens, reauthorize, and the attempt to exchange the request tokens for access tokens will have to be made again.

Listing 5.3

```php
01. <?php
02. $api_key = 'KEY_PROVIDED_BY_TWITTER_APP';
03. $api_secret = 'SECRET_PROVIDED_BY_TWITTER_APP';
04.
05. // The tokens from the authorization call. Usually retrieved from a database or session.
06. $access_token = 'CONSUMER_TOKEN';
07. $access_secret = 'CONSUMER_SECRET';
08.
09. try {
10.     // Instantiate an OAuth Instance
11.     $oauth = new OAuth(
12.         $api_key, $api_secret, OAUTH_SIG_METHOD_HMACSHA1
13.     );
14.
15.     // Enable debugging if something goes wrong
16.     $oauth->enableDebug();
17.
18.     // Set the token/secret associated to our credentials
19.     $oauth->setToken($access_token, $access_secret);
20.
21.     // Make a call to a specific endpoint
22.     $base = 'https://api.twitter.com';
23.     $tweet = $oauth->fetch($base . '/1.1/statuses/show/452478223087980544.json');
24.
25.     // retrieve the response body from the last fetch call
26.     $json = json_decode($oauth->getLastResponse());
27.     var_dump($json);
28. } catch (OAuthException $e) {
29.     echo $e->getMessage();
30. }
```

This example shows you how you can use the PECL OAuth extension to make requests once you have valid access tokens. You'll notice I didn't put my actual tokens in the code snippet. This is of course by design, because I don't want you to have them; you'll need to replace the placeholders with your actual keys to make this example to work.

Storing the access tokens in your persistence layer is up to you. Generally with OAuth 1.0 this is considered acceptable. However, a user can revoke the tokens at any point in time, so it's good practice to ensure these are valid before trying to make requests. If they are invalid, the user will have to go through the authorization process again before they can use your application.

ThePHPLeague OAuth 1 Client

The League of Extraordinary Packages,[3] provide "solid, well tested PHP packages using modern coding standards." Some of the best OAuth client packages are available through this project. If you're using a framework which doesn't provide a class, you should consider using theirs.

Installation

The PHP League OAuth-1 Client is available via Composer by adding the following to your composer.json:

```
{
    "require": {
        "league/oauth1-client": "~1.0"
    }
}
```

or use Composer to add it:

```
composer require league/oauth1-client:~1.0
```

Run composer install and you're ready to start using it. Remember to include Composer's autoloader in your script.

Obtaining and Exchanging Tokens

The PHP League offers an OAuth 1 Client package which will build the signatures and facilitate the exchange of temporary credentials for access tokens. It also provides a few specific classes for commonly used service providers. In this example, we'll look at how to retrieve temporary credentials and exchange them for access tokens.

To register for using the Tumblr API visit https://www.tumblr.com/oauth/apps

Listing 5.4

```
01. <?php
02. /**
03.  * The example was extrapolated from http://bit.ly/1NMkkLE
04.  */
05.
06. use League\OAuth1\Client\Server\Tumblr;
07.
08. // assumes were in same dir as vendor.
09. require __DIR__ . '/vendor/autoload.php';
10.
11.
```

[3]   https://thephpleague.com

```
12.  // create our server instance this is where we are going to provide the expected secrets.
13.  $server = new Tumblr([ 'identifier' => 'your-identifier',
14.                         'secret' => 'your-secret',
15.                         'callback_uri' => 'http://127.0.0.1:8080/',
16.  ]);
17.
18.  // you'll want to start a session to store request tokens
19.  session_start();
20.
21.  if (empty($_GET)) {
22.      // we'll attempt to retrieve the temporary credentials
23.      $tmpCreds = $server->getTemporaryCredentials();
24.      $_SESSION['temp_credentials'] = serialize($tmpCreds);
25.      session_write_close();
26.
27.      // once we have them we'll go to tumblr to authorize
28.      $server->authorize($tmpCreds);
29.  }
30.  /**
31.
32.  /**
33.   * The script where we get the request tokens is often the same as the callback and we'll
34.   * control what we are trying to do with some straight-forward logic statements. Since
35.   * we're expecting an oauth token and identifier to be returned, let's check for that.
36.   */
37.  if (isset($_GET['oauth_token']) && isset($_GET['oauth_verifier'])) {
38.      $tmpCreds = unserialize($_SESSION['temp_credentials']);
39.      $accessTokens = $server->getTokenCredentials(
40.          $tmpCreds, $_GET['oauth_token'], $_GET['oauth_verifier']
41.      );
42.
43.      // we'll get rid of the temporary credentials now that we have access tokens
44.      unset($_SESSION['temporary_credentials']);
45.      $_SESSION['access_tokens'] = serialize($accessTokens);
46.      session_write_close();
47.  }
```

Creating the Signature

So far, we've seen how we can retrieve our access tokens from the service we want to use with the OAuth1-Client library. Once we have our tokens, all we really need to do is create a signature with those tokens. Once we have the signature, we unlock all the protected content we have access to through an API. The next listing shows how we'd go about using this library to generate our signature.

Listing 5.5

```php
01. <?php
02. use League\OAuth1\Client\Signature\HmacSha1Signature;
03. use League\OAuth1\Client\Server\Tumblr;
04. // assumes were in same dir as vendor.
05. require __DIR__ .'/vendor/autoloac.php';
06.
07. /**
08.  * An example of how to generate a signature once our temporary credentials have been
09.  * exchanged for access tokens. We're going to assume that our access tokens and client
10.  * credentials have been serialized and persisted in a session for this example.
11.  */
12. session_start();
13. /**
14.  * The credential object is what is retrieved here, it has an interface that allows us
15.  * to call getIdentifier() and getSecret()
16.  */
17. $server = new Tumblr([ 'identifier' => 'your-identifier',
18.                        'secret' => 'your-secret',
19.                        'callback_uri' => 'http://127.0.0.1:8080/']);
20.
21. $clientCreds = $server->getClientCredentials();
22. $accessTokens = unserialize($_SESSION['access_tokens']);
23.
24. $signature = new HmacSha1Signature($clientCreds);
25. $signature->setCredentials($accessTokens);
26.
27. $parameters = [ 'oauth_nonce' => 'nonce value',
28.                 'oauth_timestamp' => time(),
29.                 'oauth_version' => '1.0',
30.                 'oauth_consumer_key' => $clientCreds->getIdentifier(),
31.                 'oauth_token' => $accessTokens->getIdentifier() ];
32.
33. $hmacsha1Signature = $signature->sign('http://127.0.0.1:8080/', $parameters,
34.                                       $method = 'POST');
```

As you can see here, we're able to take the credentials we received and build the OAuth signature. The OAuth signature, as discussed in earlier chapters, is how you actually identify yourself to the application or API you are trying to hit. Generating it is important, and as you can see here, it's really pretty easy to do. The sign method will take care of ensuring our parameters are in the proper order. All that we have to do in this case is provide all the additional parameters to the sign method. We can insert this signature in our Authorization header with all the other information, and we're good to go.

Frameworks

Frameworks have become an important part of the PHP ecosystem and provide a lot of functionality out of the box. By providing implementations which solve common problems, many programmers can find most of what they need right within the framework. Programmers tend to choose frameworks based on how familiar they are with them and how well they meet the needs of the project.

With Composer's rise in popularity, it has become less important for a framework to provide a comprehensive set of tools as they have in the past. OAuth is one of these important features frameworks are starting to move away from. As the number of high quality, standalone libraries grow, it becomes unnecessary for a framework library to compete with an existing library of high repute. That said, there are a few examples where frameworks have provided OAuth functionality in the past. While we won't spend a lot of time on these, it's beneficial to highlight them.

Zend Framework 1

Zend Framework 1[4] is still used by a large number of projects, despite a newer version being available. It provides `Zend_OAuth` as a way to deal situations where you would need to authenticate this way. The code for `Zend_OAuth` can be found at the `library/Zend/OAuth` in the project directory on GitHub. This library provides the ability to perform the token exchange, create the signature, and build the complete Authorization header. The most recent documentation for Zend Framework work is the Documentation Page[5] and describes all the classes the package is comprised of.

Zend Framework 2

Zend Framework 2[6], unlike its predecessor, does not maintain an OAuth package in their library. If you are a Zend Framework 2 user and you are looking to add OAuth functionality to use in your project, you'll need to find an existing library that fits your needs. If you are using any of the Zend products and are looking to build APIs, they provide a service called Apigility[7] which takes the difficulty out of building APIs. Apigility provides OAuth 2.0 authentication, however it does not include OAuth 1.0 authentication. Apigility will be covered in greater detail in the OAuth 2.0 chapters.

Symfony

Symfony also does not provide any OAuth functionality packaged with the framework. There is a Symfony bundle created by the Friends of Symfony,[8] but it only supports OAuth 2. If you really need an OAuth 1 package, I would suggest looking at Packagist[9] and finding the package which works best for you. If you do go the Packagist route, try to find a package with tests and a good number of installs. HWI OAuth Bundle[10] is a good candidate to examine.

[4]   https://github.com/zendframework/zf1
[5]   http://framework.zend.com/apidoc/1.12
[6]   https://github.com/zendframework/zf2
[7]   http://www.apigility.org
[8]   https://github.com/FriendsOfSymfony/
[9]   http://packagist.org
[10]   https://packagist.org/packages/hwi/oauth-bundle

Service Providers

Now that we've covered some existing libraries and you have a little better idea of how the Auth flow works for OAuth 1, let's get to the good stuff! Knowing how to get access tokens is certainly important, but it doesn't help us if we need to retrieve a tweet, a Flickr photo, an Evernote, or information from Netflix or Vimeo.

This section provides actual code which will do a number of these things. Some of these APIs are rather large, so it would be impossible for me to show you how to do every task. In every subsection, I will provide a link to the API documentation and my hope is I show enough for you to make sense of anything which isn't explicitly demonstrated.

Twitter

Twitter is one of the more commonly used services on the web today and they require the use of OAuth 1 to access their data. For these examples, we're going to be using Snaggle[11] to build the OAuth headers. For these examples, to install Snaggle and Guzzle with Composer use:

```
composer require mfrost503/snaggle
composer require guzzlehttp/guzzle
```

We'll go go through a few examples:

- how to retrieve a status,
- how to retrieve a direct message,
- how to post a status,
- and how to look at the retweets of a given status.

Before we do any of that though, let's look at how to get our request tokens and how to exchange those for access tokens.

Making the Token Exchange

The idea behind this is pretty simple:

1. Make a signed request for request tokens.
2. Redirect the user to Twitter to verify the application.
3. Send a signed request to retrieve the access tokens.

That's pretty much all it is, but we've really only looked at requests where we have the access tokens already. The signature is obviously a little bit different before the access tokens are obtained, but luckily it's a few minor changes. We still need to pass the `oauth_token` even thought it's empty, and we also have to send the same callback URL which was registered with our application. Also, as a practical note, if you don't have a site where you want to actually play with sending requests, you can use your local host files to set an actual URL as a callback (I used `http://oauth.dev` mapped to a Vagrant VM). Listing 5.6 shows how to make the token exchange.

---

[11]   https://github.com/mfrost503/Snaggle

Listing 5.6

```php
01. <?php
02. use \Snaggle\Client\Credentials\ConsumerCredentials;
03. use \Snaggle\Client\Credentials\AccessCredentials;
04. use \Snaggle\Client\Signatures\HmacSha1;
05. use \Snaggle\Client\Header\Header;
06.
07. require_once 'vendor/autoload.php';
08.
09. session_start();
10.
11. // generally, these are stored in a configuration file to re-use across your application.
12. $api_key = 'API_KEY';
13. $api_secret = 'API_SECRET';
14.
15. $consumer = new ConsumerCredentials($api_key, $api_secret);
16.
17. if (!isset($_GET['oauth_token']) && !isset($_GET['oauth_verifier'])) {
18.     $access = new AccessCredentials();
19.     $signature = new HmacSha1($consumer, $access);
20.
21.     // for testing, this can be a domain in your hosts file or even 127.0.0.1. This
22.     // assumes the file is named callback.php
23.     $signature->setCallback('http://127.0.0.1:8080/callback.php');
24.     $signature->setResourceURL('https://api.twitter.com/oauth/request_token');
25.     $signature->setHttpMethod('post');
26.
27.     $headers = new Header();
28.     $headers->setSignature($signature);
29.     $auth = $headers->createAuthorizationHeader();
30.
31.     $client = new \GuzzleHttp\Client();
32.     $response = $client->post( 'https://api.twitter.com/oauth/request_token', [
33.         'headers' => ['Authorization' => $auth]
34.     ]);
35.
36.     $res = $response->getBody();
37.     parse_str($res);
38.     $url = 'https://api.twitter.com/oauth/authorize';
39.     header("Location: {$url}?oauth_token={$oauth_token}");
40.
41. } elseif(isset($_GET['oauth_token']) && isset($_GET['oauth_verifier'])) {
42.
43.     $access = new AccessCredentials($_GET['oauth_token'], $_GET['oauth_verifier']);
44.
45.     $signature = new HmacSha1($consumer, $access);
```

```
46.    $signature->setHttpMethod( post');
47.    $signature->setResourceURL 'https://api.twitter.com/oauth/access_token');
48.
49.    $headers = new Header();
50.    $headers->setSignature($signature);
51.    $auth = $headers->createAuthorizationHeader();
52.
53.    try {
54.       $client = new \GuzzleHttp\Client();
55.       $response = $c.ient->post(
56.          'https://ap .twitter.com/oauth/access_token', [
57.             'headers  => ['Authorization' => $auth],
58.             'form_params' => [ oauth_verifier' => $_GET['oauth_verifier'] ]
59.       ]);
60.    } catch (\GuzzleHttp\Except on\ClientException $ex) {
61.       // tokens expired, need to refresh
62.       Header("Location: /callback.php");
63.       exit;
64.    }
65.
66.    $res = $response->getBody()->getContents();
67.    parse_str($res, $tokens);
68.
69.    // parse_str will create keys called 'oauth_token' and 'oauth_token_secret' you will
70.    // need to store this somewhere - session, database, etc...
71.    $_SESSION['oauth_token'] = $tokens['oauth_token'];
72.    $_SESSION['oauth_token_secret'] = $tokens['oauth_token_secret'];
73. }
```

How to Retrieve a Status

Retrieving a status simply requires you to know the ID for the status you want. Once you have it handy, making the request is pretty straight forward. The script in Listing 5.7 will retrieve one; it assumes you've saved the OAuth tokens from Listing 5.6 as session variables.

Listing 5.7

```
01. <?php
02. use \Snaggle\Client\Credentials\ConsumerCredentials;
03. use \Snaggle\Client\Credentials\AccessCredentials;
04. use \Snaggle\Client\Signatures;
05. use \Snaggle\Client\Signatures\HmacSha1;
06. use \Snaggle\Client\Header\Header;
07.
08. // Make sure the autoloader is included
09. require_once 'vendor/autoload.php';
10.
11. session_start();
12.
```

```
13.  // set up the Application Credentials
14.  $api_key = 'API_KEY';
15.  $api_secret = 'API_SECRET';
16.
17.  $consumer = new ConsumerCredentials($api_key, $api_secret);
18.
19.  // set up the User Credentials
20.  $user = new AccessCredentials($_SESSION['oauth_token'], $_SESSION['oauth_token_secret']);
21.
22.  // Create the signature and set the appropriate params
23.  $signature = new HmacSha1($consumer, $user);
24.  $signature->setHttpMethod('get');
25.  $signature->setResourceURL(
26.      'https://api.twitter.com/1.1/statuses/show/454701853591093248.json'
27.  );
28.
29.  // Use the signature to build the header
30.  $headers = new Header();
31.  $headers->setSignature($signature);
32.  $authHeader = $headers->createAuthorizationHeader();
33.
34.  // Create a Guzzle Client and use the header
35.  $client = new \GuzzleHttp\Client();
36.  $response = $client->get($signature->getResourceURL(), [
37.      'headers' => ['Authorization' => $authHeader]
38.  ]);
39.
40.  // Decode the json that comes back into an array and dump it
41.  $status = json_decode($response->getBody(), true);
42.  var_dump($status);
```

How to Retrieve a Direct Message

Retrieving a direct message involves the same process as retrieving a tweet. The only difference is the call is made to a different end point. Rather than do the exact same thing in this code snippet, we'll retrieve our last 20 direct messages. There's really nothing more to it than with the other process, but there is a difference in how we would approach it from an application standpoint. Let's assume we wanted to get a direct message, we know it was recent, but don't have the ID handy. We could query for the last 20 direct messages and parse through those to find the direct message we wanted. If we needed to, we could even pull the ID from the one we needed and make a separate request for that resource. Listing 5.8 shows how to retrieve a series of direct messages.

Listing 5.8

```php
01. <?php
02. use \Snaggle\Client\Credentials\ConsumerCredentials;
03. use \Snaggle\Client\Credentials\AccessCredentials;
04. use \Snaggle\Client\Header\Header;
05. use \Snaggle\Client\Signatures\HmacSha1;
06.
07. require_once 'vendor/autoload.php';
08.
09. session_start();
10.
11. $api_key = 'API_KEY';
12. $api_secret = 'API_SECRET';
13.
14. $consumer = new ConsumerCredentials($api_key, $api_secret);
15.
16. // set up the User Credentials
17. $user = new AccessCredentials($_SESSION['oauth_token'], $_SESSION['oauth_token_secret']);
18. $signature = new HmacSha1($consumer, $user);
19. $signature->setHttpMethod('get');
20. $signature->setResourceURL('https://api.twitter.com/1.1/direct_messages.json');
21.
22. $headers = new Header($signature);
23. $headers->setSignature($signature);
24. $authHeader = $headers->createAuthorizationHeader();
25.
26. $client = new \GuzzleHttp\Client();
27. $response = $client->get($signature->getResourceURL(), [
28.         'headers' => ['Authorization' => $authHeader]
29. ]);
30.
31. $status = json_decode($response->getBody(), true);
32. var_dump($status);
```

As you can see, we now get a list of 20 direct messages back from the API. Once we use json_decode to convert them to PHP objects, we can iterate through them and look for specific names or keywords of interest. If you aren't searching for a keyword or name, we can simply format all the direct messages into a nice clean output and peruse the whole list in a way that's easier to consume. Conversely, you could also add a ?count=30 query string to the call if you wanted to retrieve more or less than the default 20 at a time.

How to Post a Status

Posting statuses to an external social network like Facebook or twitter is an extremely common practice in many applications today. By allowing a user to post a status from your application, you can actually craft the status and allow the user to push a single button to tweet a glowing, flowery message on behalf of your application. It works well, because it doesn't inconvenience the user much, and if they've had a great experience with your application, they might be willing to send the tweet.

From a technical perspective, we're going to shift gears here. The previous examples were nice, easy ways of sending a GET request and they scale across the entire API. Sending a message is a little bit different, it requires us to send a POST request. While there are some differences, they're easily navigated (see Listing 5.9).

Listing 5.9

```php
01. <?php
02. use \Snaggle\Client\Credentials\ConsumerCredentials;
03. use \Snaggle\Client\Credentials\AccessCredentials;
04. use \Snaggle\Client\Signatures;
05. use \Snaggle\Client\Signatures\HmacSha1;
06. use \Snaggle\Client\Header\Header;
07.
08. // Make sure the autoloader is included
09. require_once 'vendor/autoload.php';
10.
11. session_start();
12.
13. // set up the Application Credentials
14. $api_key = 'API_KEY';
15. $api_secret = 'API_SECRET';
16. $consumer = new ConsumerCredentials($api_key, $api_secret);
17.
18. // set up the User Credentials
19. $user = new AccessCredentials($_SESSION['oauth_token'], $_SESSION['oauth_token_secret']);
20.
21. $signature = new HmacSha1($consumer, $user);
22. $signature->setHttpMethod('POST');
23. $signature->setResourceURL('https://api.twitter.com/1.1/statuses/update.json');
24. $signature->setPostFields(['status' => rawurlencode('Test Tweet For OAuth')]);
25.
26. $headers = new Header($signature);
27. $headers->setSignature($signature);
28. $authHeader = $headers->createAuthorizationHeader();
29.
30. $client = new \GuzzleHttp\Client();
31. $response = $client->post( $signature->getResourceURL(), [
32.     'headers' => ['Authorization' => $authHeader],
33.     'form_params' => ['status' => 'Test Tweet For OAuth']
34. ]);
```

```
35. $status = json_decode($response->getBody(), true);
36. var_dump($status);
```

One minor difference here is when we're sending a post request, any fields which are required as part of the call must be added to the base string. The other slightly annoying part of this is the values have to be double encoded. So for instance, when a space is encoded once it becomes %20 and when a percent sign is encoded once it becomes %25. In practice this means if you have a space in your tweet (a fairly common occurrence), any spaces will no longer need to be encoded as %20, they'll need to be %2520. If you are using a library, they should be handling this for you, but it's definitely important to know if you are writing your own request. Since it's in the base string, the server side will use the tweet in the body to verify the signature. If you get it wrong, you'll receive a 401 status and not much else.

How to View Retweets

At this point, we've covered a number of common tasks, the last thing we're going to take a look at is seeing the retweets for any given tweet. It's always exciting when you tweet something and it gets retweeted by a lot of people. Perhaps you want to see who all those people are without using a common Twitter client. This endpoint will give you a ton of information about the retweets and the users behind them.

Listing 5.10

```
01. <?php
02. use \Snaggle\Client\Credentials\ConsumerCredentials;
03. use \Snaggle\Client\Credentials\AccessCredentials;
04. use \Snaggle\Client\Signatures\HmacSha1;
05. use \Snaggle\Client\Header\Header;
06.
07. require_once 'vendor/autoload.php';
08.
09. session_start();
10.
11. $api_key = 'API_KEY';
12. $api_secret = 'API_SECRET';
13.
14. $api_key = 'YOUR KEY';
15. $api_secret = 'YOUR APPLICATION SECRET';
16.
17. $consumer = new ConsumerCredentials($api_key, $api_secret);
18.
19. // set up the User Credentials
20. $user = new AccessCredentials($_SESSION['oauth_token'], $_SESSION['oauth_token_secret']);
21.
22. $signature = new HmacSha1($consumer, $user);
23. $signature->setHttpMethod('get');
24. $signature->setResourceURL(
25.     'https://api.twitter.com/1.1/statuses/retweets.json?id=454701853591093248'
26. );
```

```
27.
28.  // Use the signature to build the header
29.  $headers = new Header();
30.  $headers->setSignature($signature);
31.  $authHeader = $headers->createAuthorizationHeader();
32.
33.  $client = new \GuzzleHttp\Client();
34.  $response = $client->get($signature->getResourceURL(), [
35.      'headers' => [ 'Authorization' => $authHeader ],
36.  ]);
37.
38.  $status = json_decode($response->getBody(), true);
39.  var_dump($status);
```

As you can see, there isn't a whole lot to it once the headers are created, you can simply send your requests and the headers along with them and unlock a ton of data.

Tumblr

Tumblr is a popular blogging service that's been around since 2007 and has an OAuth 1.0 API. We're going to look at a couple of different calls here with Tumblr to get the feel for making a call and getting our access tokens. Before we get too far into it though, we did use Snaggle again for our examples to avoid having to write the signature and header code repeatedly. We know how those all work now, so it shouldn't be difficult.

> To register an application for accessing the Tumblr API, go to
> https://www.tumblr.com/oauth/register

The first thing we will look at is the OAuth token flow. This is pretty straight forward, however, Tumblr does something Twitter does not do. When we get our very first request tokens, an oauth_token_secret is sent back with it. As you know, once we get the token we have to authorize the application. That means we're going to have to find a way to persist the secret and retrieve it when we make our call for the access tokens. For the sake of resources and simplicity, I wrote the secret to a file on the file system, see Listing 5.11. If you are using this process in any production related system, you should store it in a database and associate it with the user authorizing your script's access to their Tumblr data.

Listing 5.11

```
01.  <?php
02.  use Snaggle\Client\Credentials\ConsumerCredentials;
03.  use Snaggle\Client\Credentials\AccessCredentials;
04.  use Snaggle\Client\Signatures\HmacSha1;
05.  use Snaggle\Client\Header\Header;
06.
07.  require_once 'vendor/autoload.php';
08.
09.  session_start();
```

```php
10.  // set up the Application Credentials
11.  $api_key = 'API_KEY';
12.  $api_secret = 'API_SECRET';
13.
14.  $consumer = new ConsumerCredentials($api_key, $api_secret);
15.
16.  $access = new AccessCredentials();
17.  $client = new \GuzzleHttp\Client();
18.
19.  if (!isset($_GET['oauth_token']) && !isset($_GET['oauth_callback_confirmed'])) {
20.      $signature = new HmacSha1($consumer, $access);
21.      // You will need to change this value to point to your actual callback endpoint
22.      $signature->setCallback('http://127.0.0.1:8080/');
23.      $signature->setHttpMethod('POST');
24.      $signature->setResourceURL('http://www.tumblr.com/oauth/request_token');
25.
26.      $header = new Header();
27.      $header->setSignature($signature);
28.      $auth = $header->createAuthorizationHeader();
29.      $response = $client->post('http://www.tumblr.com/oauth/request_token', [
30.          'headers' => ['Authorization' => $auth]
31.      ]);
32.      $body = $response->getBody()->getContents();
33.      parse_str($body, $tokens);
34.
35.      // I'm using a file write for persistence of the token secret, for the sake of example.
36.      // You should use something more secure.
37.      $fh = fopen('token.txt', 'w');
38.      fwrite($fh, $tokens['oauth_token_secret']);
39.      fclose($fh);
40.
41.      $authorize = 'http://www.tumblr.com/oauth/authorize?oauth_token='
42.                  . $tokens['oauth_token'];
43.      header("Location: $authorize");
44.  } elseif (isset($_GET['oauth_verifier']) && isset($_GET['oauth_token'])) {
45.      // this is to simulate what a read from your persistence layer would be like
46.      $fh = fopen('token.txt', 'r');
47.      $data = fread($fh, 1024);
48.      fclose($fh);
49.
50.      $access = new AccessCredentials($_GET['oauth_token'], $data);
51.      $signature = new HmacSha1($consumer, $access);
52.      $signature->setHttpMethod('POST');
53.      $signature->setResourceURL('http://www.tumblr.com/oauth/access_token');
54.      $signature->setVerifier($_GET['oauth_verifier']);
55.      // You will need to change this value to point to your actual callback endpoint
56.      $signature->setCallback('http://127.0.0.1:8080/index2.php');
```

```
57.
58.    $header = new Header();
59.    $header->setSignature($signature);
60.    $auth = $header->createAuthorizationHeader();
61.    $response = $client->post('http://www.tumblr.com/oauth/access_token', [
62.        'headers' => ['Authorization' => $auth]
63.    ]);
64.
65.    $body = $response->getBody();
66.    parse_str($body, $tokens);
67.
68.    // I'm using a file write for persistence of the token secret, for the sake of example.
69.    // You should use something more secure.
70.    $fh = fopen('token.txt', 'w');
71.    fwrite($fh, $tokens['oauth_token_secret']);
72.    fclose($fh);
73.
74.    // save tokens in $_SESSION
75.    $_SESSION['oauth_token'] = $tokens['oauth_token'];
76.    $_SESSION['oauth_token_secret'] = $tokens['oauth_token_secret'];
77. }
```

As you might imagine, all the dirty work there is done. We have our tokens and we can now get ready to use them to make a simple call to the Tumblr API. This particular call is going to retrieve user information. As you might suspect, it's not complicated once we have all our credentials.

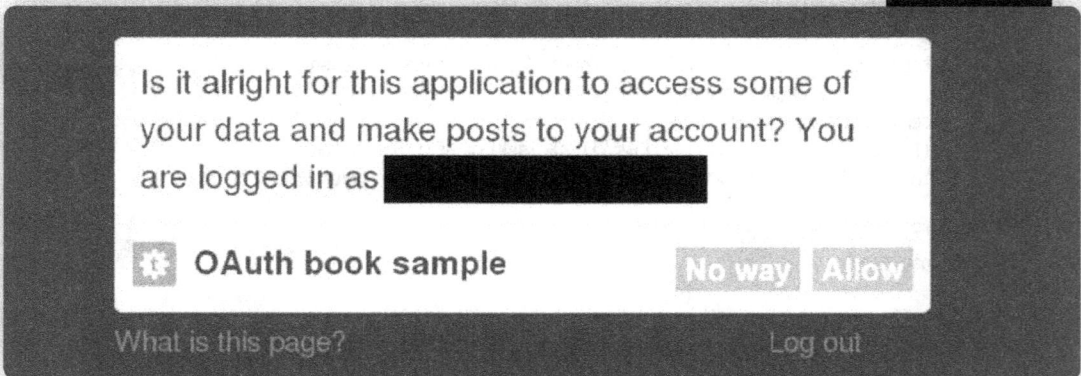

FIGURE 5.3

Listing 5.12 gives an even better understanding how to sign and make OAuth 1.0 requests. If you wanted to make this even easier, you could actually use the Tumblr Client[12] they provide on their GitHub account. It's a very simple, lightweight API wrapper which prevents you from having to write all the request code.

Listing 5.12

```php
01. <?php
02. use \Snaggle\Client\Credentials\ConsumerCredentials;
03. use \Snaggle\Client\Credentials\AccessCredentials;
04. use \Snaggle\Client\Signatures\HmacSha1;
05. use \Snaggle\Client\Header\Header;
06.
07. require_once 'vendor/autoload.php';
08.
09. session_start();
10.
11. // set up the Application Credentials
12. $api_key = 'API_KEY';
13. $api_secret = 'API_SECRET';
14.
15. $consumer = new ConsumerCredentials($api_key, $api_secret);
16.
17. $access = new AccessCredentials($_SESSION['oauth_token'],
18.                                 $_SESSION['oauth_token_secret']);
19.
20. $resource = 'http://api.tumblr.com/v2/user/info';
21.
22. $signature = new HmacSha1($consumer, $access);
23. $signature->setHttpMethod('GET');
24. $signature->setResourceURL($resource);
25.
26. $header = new Header();
27. $header->setSignature($signature);
28. $auth = $header->createAuthorizationHeader();
29.
30. $client = new \GuzzleHttp\Client();
31. $response = $client->get($signature->getResourceURL(), [
32.     'headers' => ['Authorization' => $auth]
33. ]);
34.
35. $data = $response->getBody()->getContents();
36. $user_info = json_decode($data);
37.
38. var_dump($user_info);
```

[12] https://github.com/tumblr/tumblr.php

Summary

Even with a thorough understanding of OAuth 1.0, it still may be necessary to dig through the documentation for the service you are trying to use. Not all services use the same format for the base string, despite it being quite clear in the specification. Having an understanding of the process of signing a request goes a long way, from there you'll only have to figure out what's different for each service. If the documentation is up to snuff, you should have no problem taking this knowledge and applying to integrate OAuth 1.0 services into your project.

This chapter has shed light on the mysterious world of OAuth 1.0. The examples are here for you to draw from, experiment with, and modify in order to meet your needs. As we've discussed, the signature is the most complex piece of the puzzle. Once you understand how to build those for the services you want to use, it should be smooth sailing from there.

Chapter
6

OAuth 2 Client

We've taken a close look at OAuth 1 clients; this chapter will focus on the OAuth 2 client. OAuth 2 provides solutions for the same type of authorization problems OAuth 1 solves, it just does it in a slightly different manner. OAuth 2 is really more of a framework than a single protocol.

There are times when we'll want to pull user content or resources from a third-party site into our application. For reasons described earlier, we don't want to have to manage, store, or know our user's credentials; nor do we want to have provide those credentials to a third-party service whenever we want their content. Doing this puts an unreasonable responsibility on us to ensure we're the only other people who know these user name and password combinations.

In addition, our users are not going to be happy if they have to change the credentials for a single service on more than one site. Happy, well protected users are going to ensure they continue to use our application and aren't scared away because of security or inconvenience.

Authorization Flow

In OAuth 2 we still rely on the individual external services to be primarily responsible for user name and password security. The process differs a little bit from OAuth 1, but still requires an exchange between an application and the service. In OAuth 2 we eliminate the need for signatures, which are one of the more difficult concepts in OAuth 1. Instead we swap out the use of signatures and instead use encrypted information over SSL. Without SSL, we don't have OAuth 2, so keep that in mind when considering implementing OAuth 2. Figure 6.1 illustrates the basic workflow involved in OAuth 2.0.

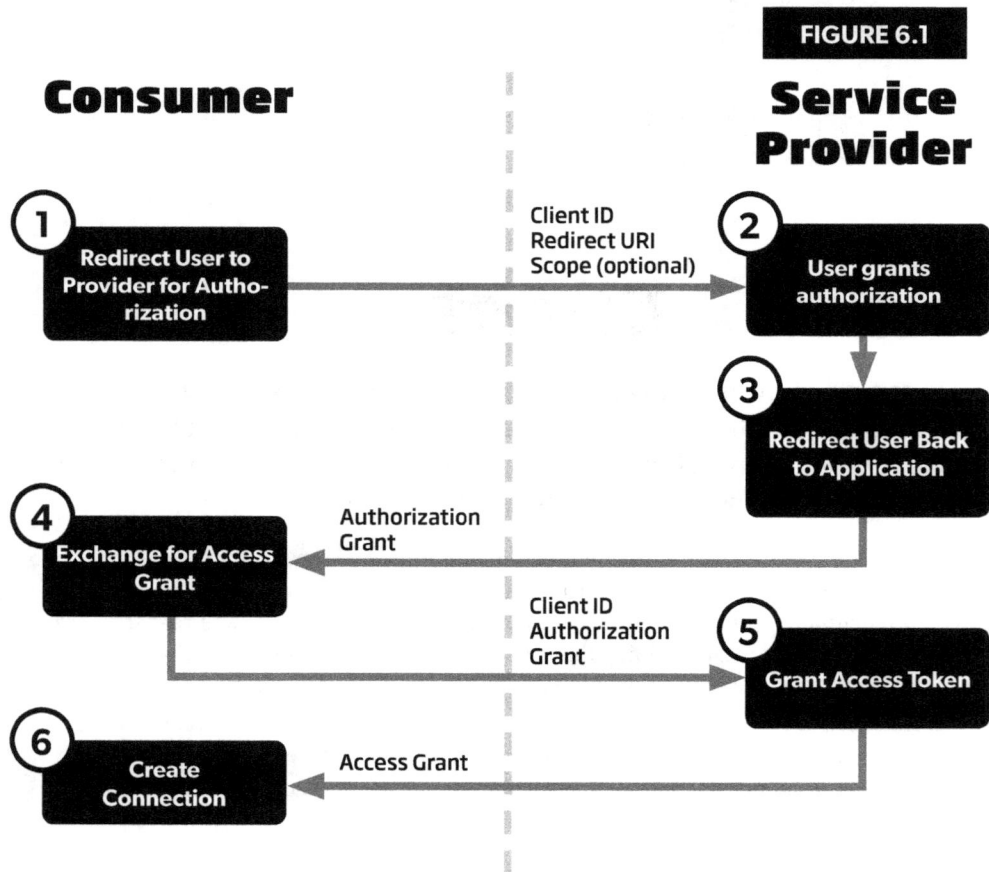

FIGURE 6.1

The first thing we need to do is create an authorization request and send it to the server. This is generally a link we can redirect our users to which allows them to authenticate with the third-party application and allows our application to interact with their account. If this is successful, the application will send an *Authorization Grant* back to us. This tells us the user authenticated successfully and we can proceed to the next step. Once we have a successful authentication and authorization, we'll need to exchange that grant for an *access token*. The access token identifies us to the third party server, so it's important for these steps to flow together to ensure we're being identified correctly. Once we have an access token (which can expire very quickly when compared to OAuth 1 access tokens), we can provide it in our requests to retrieve information from the third-party service.

Another change introduced is the idea of a *refresh token*. A refresh token is not a required part of OAuth 2, which means you should check to determine whether the service you are integrating with offers them. The idea behind the refresh token is if credentials expire, the application should alert you the tokens you provided are not valid (via an appropriate response and status code). At that point, a request providing the refresh token can be made in order to request a new access token. The **only** use for a refresh token is to request a new token, so it's part of the authorization and not a part of the retrieval, removal, or modification of resources. To reiterate, *this is not a required piece of OAuth 2*, so verify the service you wish to use offers refresh tokens. If it does not, you'll have to go through the normal authorization process again in order to obtain a new token when an access token expires.

There's really not much else to it, the crux of the authorization framework is an exchange takes place and consistently identifies us correctly. Going forward, we need to ensure we provide our proof of identification–the access token–in a way the server is expecting so it knows how to authorize us when dealing with protected content.

Before you start thinking, "Wow that's it? This is going to be a really short chapter", there are a number of new concepts we're going to have to comprehend in order to fully understand how this all works together.

Scopes

If you're like me, you've always wondered why OAuth 1 was so difficult to understand, yet did very little to help solve the always tricky authorization problem. Authorization, in short, is making sure your users can see what they're allowed to see and not allowing unauthorized users to see the same protected content. Obviously, protected content and how it is defined differs from application to application, but in short, someone who isn't me or a person I've authorized (by friending, following, etc) shouldn't be able to see my files, likes, pictures, and so on. Due to the variant nature of applications, it would be very difficult to come up with a universal access control system which would work for everyone. It would be so difficult and the implications of failure could be so disastrous, it's really not even worth attempting.

OAuth 2 can, however, provide more control over what is available to an authenticated user in a given application. I'm sure we've all seen an authorization page which asks us if we want to connect to this application, but if you look closely it will also tell you what the application has access to. Consider Twitter as an example, you have read or read-write access across the board. Your application can either read all the protected resources or read and create content in all the protected resources. This might be acceptable for your application, but how would we handle restricting users from accessing direct messages? Long story short, we can't.

Scopes can allow the application to determine what specific resources the access token is authorized to use, and how they are authorized to use them. Keep in mind, the application is still responsible for building the mechanisms to manage these scopes, so it's still something you would have to consider when using or building with OAuth 2. Basically, we're exchanging the model of "read and/or write everything" for a more specific model which asks, "what do you want to have read and/or write access to?". As a prime example, take a look at the GitHub API; they require scopes when requesting access tokens and have a pretty detailed list of the resources you can manage. GitHub provides the following scopes:

- user
- user:email
- user:follow
- public_repo
- repo
- repo_deployment,
- repo:status
- delete_repo
- read:org
- write:org
- read:public_key
- write:public_key

This isn't the complete list; it can be found at GitHub API Scopes[1].

From the few I chose to detail, you can see a much finer level of access control managed with the tokens. It's very likely the management of public keys or the ability to delete repositories might not be something your application really wants users to do. By providing a list of scopes when you make your authorization request, you can effectively limit the use of the API to perform those actions. In a sense, it provides a little bit more clarity to the authorization flow and how it can be managed on the server.

Scopes are only used in the process where we are retrieving tokens and can (but don't have to) be used in the generation of the actual access token. Any calls which made to protected resources do not require those scopes to be passed along or maintained from call to call. They become strictly part of the authorization and authentication process. The service provider will verify the scopes allowed for any given access token.

We've taken a cursory look at how the authentication flow works, but as you might suspect, there's more to it than that. We're starting to approach usability, but it's important to understand the specifics on how we retrieve our access tokens, what implications it might have, and–if we have a choice–when to use which type of grant. We're going to be covering that next.

[1]   *Github API Scopes:* https://developer.github.com/v3/oauth/#scopes

Grants

Up to this point, we've covered this whole authentication flow process from a really basic standpoint. While it's good to understand the basic flow of things, it's equally important to understand the specific mechanisms which make this flow work. In this section, we're going to cover the grants we can use to retrieve our access token. If you recall from he OAuth 1 Client chapter, we were given an access token and an access secret. We needed both to build the signature. In this model, we're only going to be retrieving one token, the idea of the access secret goes away. Because of this, don't be surprised if you are unable to see the actual access token in the third party application settings. This token should be be treated with the same sensitivity as a password and not be shared with the world at large.

Authorization Code Grant

The authorization code grant can be used to obtain both access tokens and refresh tokens. This grant is what most people think of when they think of OAuth because it requires a callback and returns a token once the process is completed. This grant requires the user to authenticate with the third-party service directly before continuing. Once the token is retrieved, it can be stored by the calling application and used to make future requests as long as the token is valid.

To break down how this grant works in practice, let's step through the complete process. The third-party service provides an authorization endpoint and the user is directed there. The endpoint, according to the OAuth 2 RFC[2], must have a response type which is set to code and a client ID. The redirect_uri option is regarded as optional documentation for the service you are trying to use and will often provide more information about the callback. If your service uses scopes, this is the step where you'd provide them. If there are multiple scopes, as in our GitHub example, they can be provided as a comma-delimited list. Finally, there is an option called state, which is regarded as recommended because it acts as a protection against Cross-Site Request Forgery attacks. The state is passed back by the authorization server after the request is made. This acts as a way to ensure the request wasn't altered while en route. Here's an example of how we'd build a request for GitHub, assuming we'd like our key to have scope for user:follow, public_repo, and read:org.

```
https://github.com/login/oauth/authorize?client_id=CLIENT_ID
&response_type=code&scope=user follow,public_repo,read:org
&redirect_uri=http://example.com/callback&state=bced12345ace
```

When a user visits this link from your application, completes his or her login, and gives your application access to his or her account, your application will receive a temporary code. This is generally done as a redirect to the callback with a code in the query string. This temporary code will be used as a required parameter to obtain an access token. It's short-lived, so you'll have to move the process forward within a reasonable amount of time.

Once you obtain your temporary code, you'll have to make a POST request to the access token endpoint. The body of that POST request must contain the following fields: grant_type, code, redirect_uri, and client_id. The grant type you would use for the Authorization Code grant

[2]   RFC 6749, https://tools.ietf.org/html/rfc6749

is `authorization_code`. The code is the temporary value you retrieved from the authorization step. If the `redirect_uri` was provided in the authorization step, it must be identical to the callback in the first request; it is a required field during this step. Finally, the `client_id`, which helps identify your application, must be sent over as well. If this is sent correctly, you will be redirected to the callback with an access token. If the service provides a refresh token, it can also be provided at this point. Now, you'll have an access token and be able to authenticate and authorize requests to protected resources on the third-party application.

Implicit Grant

The Implicit Grant is a little bit different than the Authorization Code Grant. The process starts out the same, where the user is directed to an authorization endpoint where they will login with their credentials. Once authenticated, the user will be redirected, but the access token is provided on the first redirection. There is no temporary code exchange required to retrieve the access token.

While there are fewer steps in this process, it should generally only be used in situations where the access token cannot be stored securely. This token should be treated as public knowledge, and it's advisable to not allow any overly destructive permissions to be carried out via this token. The Implicit Grant also doesn't allow for refresh tokens to be distributed, since they would be potentially publicly available as well. In order to retrieve new tokens, the authorization process must be completed again.

Resource Owner Password Credentials Grant

In the last two grants, we've seen how we've been redirected to the third-party website to authenticate and authorize the application. This third kind of grant does not utilize redirection at all and is therefore pretty scary to consider using. In fact, the RFC states it should only be used when there isn't a viable alternative. In this scenario a POST request is made to the authorization server and the following fields **must** be present in the request: `grant_type` set to `'password'`, `username`, and `password`. Additionally, scopes can be set the same way as described earlier in the chapter. The authorization server is required to only store the sent credentials until an access token is provided, at which point it cannot store them. Keep in mind, this requirement is only in place to remain OAuth 2 compliant, there is no actual mechanism forcing the server to remove your credentials.

You can probably see how scary this is, just based on the fact you are sending your username and password. The specification requires this POST request to be sent over with Transport Layer Security (TLS). But keep in mind this sends your user's password directly in the request.

I just want to take another opportunity to be cautious when considering this grant. The reason is simple: tokens are generally short-lived and easily revoked. If a token is compromised, it can be invalidated very quickly. When a password is compromised, a user is open to all the same issues as a compromised token. In addition, the attacker now has access to the user's account on the third-party service. This could allow for passwords to be changed and accounts to be hi-jacked. Only use this grant in a situation where there is an extremely high level of trust and even then only if you absolutely must.

While it can be dangerous, it is a valid grant type in OAuth 2 and it's important to understand some of the concerns associated with using it. With any application, it's very important to follow secure password practices in order to maintain your users' online security. Ideally, users would have longer passwords with varying character types (letters, symbols, numbers, etc.) and would not use the same password on more than one application. Any problem posed by a password being leaked out can be magnified if one password allows access to other online accounts.

Client Credential Grant

The last type of grant we'll be covering is the Client Credential Grant. Similar to the previous kind of grant, it requires the sending over of a different set of credentials. As with the previous grant, this should only be used by clients who are not public facing. When implementing this grant, the `client_id` and `client_secret` are used as opposed to the resource owner's credentials. The `client_id` and `client_secret` are the values which are used to identify the application, so it goes without saying, these values need to be protected from the outside world. They can be used for a service having no outside access, a private network for example, and where the ID and secret can be shared with little to no risk.

To use this grant, a request has to be made to the token endpoint with a parameter for the `grant_type` set to `'client_credentials'` and, optionally, a list of scopes. To send the ID and secret along, you can use an `Authorization` header which utilizes `Basic` authentication. Basic authentication is created when the identifier and secret are combined and separated by a colon. So for example if my `client_id` is `'123'` and my `client_secret` is `'abc'`, you would start with the string `'123:abc'`. This value is then base64 encoded and added to the authorization header. If those values are authenticated, then an access token is returned. Below is a value of what the *Basic Authorization* header would look like, with a place holder for the encoded value.

```
Authorization: Basic <base64 encoded identifier:secret string>
```

It's very simple; of course, since they have to be authenticated they have to be encoded and not hashed. This means anyone with access to the string can base64 decode it and get access to the original information. PHP provides a function to do this called, `base64_decode`. For this reason, I'd stress again you should only use this in confidential situations.

Presenting the Access Token

Obtaining the access token is the most involved part of this process. Unlike OAuth 1, there isn't a lot we have to do to identify ourselves to protected resources once we have it. The simplicity of OAuth 2 makes it a bit easier to use on a request to request basis. The trade off is the access tokens tend to have a much shorter life than the access credentials in OAuth 1.

The service will return a token and token type upon the successful request for access tokens. It's important to check with the service you are using to see how the service requires the token to be presented. Some services state you should put them in the URL, while others have different token types which are required for use in the Authorization header. There will be more on this in the OAuth 2 implementation chapter. For example, GitHub documentation says to use the following:

```
Authorization: token <token>
```

Other examples replace the word token with bearer and for an example of a service which states to use it as a query parameter, we can take a look at Foursquare:

```
https://api.foursquare.com/v2/users/self/checkins?oauth_token=ACCESS_TOKEN
```

There's no single way to present the token in a request. The important aspect is that it's presented in a way the resource server can access and identify the token. Always be sure to check the documentation for any differences in how to present your token. Also in addition to the examples listed above, it's possible there are other methods for presenting the tokens which are specific to a particular service.

Chapter
7

OAuth 2 Server

Now that you've seen how the <u>OAuth 1</u> process works, you may have decided you want to provide access to your content using OAuth 2. Or perhaps you already knew you wanted to use OAuth 2 and jumped straight to this chapter, that's just fine. In this chapter, we're going to look at the finer points of implementing an OAuth 2 server to serve your content. This section includes a bit on authorization, as well as authentication and the different types of grants you may want to support.

In the <u>OAuth 1 Server chapter</u>, you'll remember we had to break down and reconstruct the signature in order to authenticate the user. The good news for OAuth 2.0 is that the signature goes away completely, getting the information needed to authenticate a user is much easier. We also have a better framework for handling authorization to certain resources, which will come in handy.

SSL/TLS

So before we get into a lot of the technical details, OAuth 2 requires you communicate to the server securely. This means, as a server provider, you are going to need Transport Layer Security (TLS) or Secure Sockets Layer (SSL) to encrypt and protect the requests that are made to the server. This means that as a service provider, you are going to be responsible for obtaining and maintaining the certificates your server needs to ensure the sensitive data in incoming requests is properly encrypted and your web servers are configured to use only HTTPS for OAuth requests.

It is important to note the use of TLS/SSL is **not optional** according to the OAuth 2 specification, as it acts as a cryptographic alternative to signed requests. Since we're dealing with fewer tokens, the tokens we are using need to be handled with care and caution. More on the tokens later, the importance of this section is that you understand and can start planning for the requirement of using TLS/SSL for your OAuth 2 driven service.

Tokens and Grants

The main concept in both versions of OAuth is that a user is able to authenticate with a service and obtain an identifier which allows them to communicate with the API in a way that hides or doesn't use their user name and password. By eliminating the need to send the user name and password in each request, OAuth helps protect the credentials for the service from being hijacked from a request. Instead, OAuth uses identifiers known as tokens which can easily be regenerated and revoked in the event they are compromised. This process is a great deal more convenient than having to reset a user name and password.

In OAuth 1, these tokens are combined into a hashed signature which can be recreated to verify the identity of the user. In OAuth 2, because of the TLS/SSL requirement, the tokens are provided with the requests which makes the formation of the requests much easier to understand. This method also eliminates the need to have an access token and an access secret, favoring the access token. As a result, the implementation of an OAuth 2 server is easier to understand.

If you are using a library, there is likely already a method for generating the access token; if you can use a library method you should. If you are writing your own implementation, you need to determine the length (in characters) of the access token you generate. You also need to make sure each access token which is generated is unique from any active access tokens. Similar to how we created the nonce in OAuth 1 clients, we can create a random string like this:

```
$bytes = openssl_random_pseudo_bytes(20);
$token = bin2hex($bytes);
```

The previous code will create a hexadecimal representation of the random bytes and generate a token which is 40 characters long.

Authorization Code Grant

The first grant we are going to take a look at is the Authorization Code Grant. As the name implies, there is an authorization code which is required in order to successfully implement this grant. In order to use this grant in your server, the user will need to authenticate with your service. This usually means the user is redirected to a URL belonging to your application which allows them to authenticate and authorize the calling application. Once this happens, an authorization code needs to be generated and associated with the authenticating user. In addition to creating this authorization code and making the proper association, it's also important this token not be allowed to be valid for a long period of time. It needs to expire after a set amount of time; this can vary, but ideally a couple of minutes should be plenty of time for the user to take the next step.

Once the user has authenticated and has been redirected back to the redirect URL from the calling application, a second request has to be made. This request serves as the primary way to obtain an access token. The user will make a request for the access token by passing along the client key, client secret, Authorization Code, and the redirect URI. If everything matches and the Authorization Code has not expired, an access token is returned. In order to return one, a token needs to be created and associated with the correct user account. The access token is the primary mechanism for identifying a user. Optionally, you can choose to also return a refresh token, which will allow the user to easily recreate any token which has expired. It's important to allow the access tokens to expire after an amount of time that seems reasonable for your application and use case.

By requiring an authorization code, you are ensuring a user takes multiple steps to verify themselves to your application. This grant type should be used whenever possible, as the additional request naturally provides a layer of security and ensures requests were not hijacked and modified prior to the tokens being assigned.

Implicit Grant

The Implicit Grant provides an easy way of obtaining the access token by sending the token immediately after the user authenticates with your service. By not requiring the user to send an authorization code back to your server, access tokens can be very easily obtained by users who may not have the ability to generate a second request. This grant can be particularly useful in applications built solely with JavaScript. It's important to communicate to users the use cases where using the Implicit Grant may be advantageous.

Because there is no authorization code, the second level of verification is obviously removed. This is why having short-lived tokens is a smart strategy to employ and why this grant should only be used when the Authorization Code Grant is impermissible or overly difficult to implement. I strongly urge you to properly communicate via documentation and other necessary means the proper utilization of this grant. I'd even go a step further and indicate use of this grant should not be used as a shortcut to the Authorization Code Grant.

Ensuring you are properly deactivating tokens and taking other security precautions is an important step to ensure user data in your application remains secure and unmolested. There is a greater threat of theft when the user is not required to verify the receipt of non-access token information. While you certainly can't prevent users from misusing anything in your application, communicating clearly is your responsibility to anyone who may be using your API for their application.

Client Credential Grant

The Client Credential Grant is a grant which allows a user to authenticate to the service by providing the consumer key and secret via Basic authentication. In this grant, there really isn't a user to identify. As a result, it is important any user-related read/writes are sufficiently protected and the operations the API can perform are kept to a minimum.

In addition to keeping these permissions to a limited number of well defined operations, it's very important this grant be used when there is a high level of trust between the client and the server. This grant can be used on internal systems because the trust level is extremely high. When providing this grant type to the world at large, it's important to understand everything this application is capable of modifying and/or running. If, when providing this API, you find there are areas of the application which are unclear or jobs which may have unintended consequences ensure you obtain the knowledge of these jobs and requests prior to making this grant type available.

Resource Owner Credential Grant

The Resource Owner Credential Grant allows a user to provide their username and password combination, again via Basic auth, in exchange for an access token. This request will be associated with a user, so it is permissible for protected resources to be obtained, created, edited, or deleted. Because a username and password combination is set, it remains very important this is used only between systems with a high level of trust.

A compromised user account can be a very detrimental situation, both for the compromised user and the maintainer of the application. Passwords often need to be reset in multiple locations and credentials generally grant a larger number of acceptable operations. This token, along with the Client Credential Token should timeout after a reasonable amount of time for your application. Understanding the proper use cases and the technology behind this grant is very important if you are considering using or implementing it. While OAuth 2.0 takes steps to ensure there are multiple ways for users to retrieve access tokens, it is important to ensure the users can be sufficiently protected while they consume your service.

Refresh Token Grant

The Refresh Token Grant makes the process of obtaining new tokens much easier by providing a refresh token when the access token is obtained. Refresh tokens are not required. They are an optional part of the specification. If a refresh token is provided, it is very important it be properly protected and stored securely, by both clients and your application. If one is compromised it can allow an unauthorized user to generate new access tokens on behalf of another user.

As we've discussed, OAuth 2 access tokens tend to be shorter lived than their OAuth 1 counterparts. By encouraging short-life tokens, security improves but usability can suffer if considerations for expired tokens are not made carefully. When an access token expires, a user can send their refresh token to an endpoint which will exchange it for a new access token. In the event a refresh token is not part of the authorization flow, the user will have to authenticate with the third-party service again in order to obtain a new access token.

Access Control

When implementing any sort of server housing protected resources, authentication and authorization are vital to ensure the information is protected in the proper way. This could be, but is not necessarily limited to, ensuring users can only create, update, or delete data they have access to and ensuring users can only see data they're supposed to see. It also is vital in ensuring non-administrative users do not have access to administrative tools on the application itself. It's a problem everyone who's ever written an application has to face, and let's be frank, it's generally not a whole lot of fun.

OAuth 2.0 doesn't solve these problems directly. It's really important to understand every application is different and will have different requirements for protected resources. What this ultimately means is as an application creator, you are still responsible for maintaining the proper permissions and requirements when it comes to creating or dealing with these protected resources. While OAuth 2 doesn't directly handle this for you, there is a concept that was introduced in OAuth 2.0 that provides a jumping off point for implementing this idea. This concept is referred to as Scopes.

Scopes

Scopes provide a way for an application to identify the types of resources they'll be interacting with and the type of the access they will need to use those resources. These really only come into play with protected resources, as public resources can be handled by the API itself. Take for instance a service like Twitter, while the public time line could be accessible by anyone, they would certainly want to restrict the ability for someone to create a tweet under a certain account. The same goes for GitHub's gists and a number of other applications.

In OAuth 1.0, if you wanted to restrict the ability to create tweets from the API, you would have to set the entire application to read-only. It would also restrict the ability to create direct messages, which may or may not be what you need to do. If you want to allow the creation of direct messages, you would also have to allow the creation of tweets. This process really limits the amount of control a user has when creating a client application and potentially opens up to their application to being used in a way it wasn't intended.

Scopes allow application developers to drill down into specific resource types and set the access requirements for those types individually. Where Twitter, which uses OAuth 1.0, only allows you to set an application to read-all or write-all, GitHub can allow you to toggle read and write access to specific resources. This type of access can be requested at the time the access tokens are requested, and allows an access token to be set and properly associated with these scopes to ensure the permissions are not lost.

Scope Implementation

As I mentioned before, the work of actually enforcing these scopes still falls on the creator of the service. In an overly simplified view, the client is going to make requests to the server. It's the server's job to know whether the request is allowed, authorized, and should be fulfilled. If the client makes a request to a resource not in the list of allowable scopes, the request should be denied, with the appropriate response and status codes. It'd be improper–and frankly confusing–if the limitations and control scopes provide were to be ignored or not implemented consistently.

If you are writing a service using OAuth 2.0, an important part of planning your service will be to to know and define:

- the different types of resources available to your users,
- whether or not those resources are regarded as public or protected.

Applications are as unique and diverse as the people that write them, so it is impossible to suggest a one-size-fits-all approach. Access Control can be very difficult and mistakes in this area tend to be very costly and damaging to the reputation and credibility of an application. Scopes can be a very handy way to define the protected resources in your API or application and to ensure all the use cases for interacting with them are covered correctly and responsibly.

Conclusion

We've been able to look at some key components of an OAuth 2.0 server in depth, how the server works, and some of the differences between OAuth 1 and OAuth 2. Understanding the technology and process involved allows application and service creators to make informed decisions about the protocols and technologies they may want to use in their applications. As we've seen throughout the book, there are definitely differences between the OAuth versions from both the client and server side. By breaking down the walls of confusion, and understanding the process in simpler terms, we're able to provide solutions to common problems in a concise, separated manner.

Chapter
8

OAuth 2 Implementation

After reading the chapters associated with OAuth 2.0 and you may find yourself asking what it all means. This chapter will cover how to use a number of common OAuth 2.0 APIs. Adding this practical experience to your tool belt will allow you to integrate any number of OAuth 2.0 driven services into your application or code.

Before we really dive into this, there are a couple expectations to set about the examples provided in this chapter. For starters, I'm only going to provide one script for the retrieval of access tokens, unless it makes sense to highlight a different approach. All of the API specific examples are going to assume you have retrieved the access token from the service. For these examples I'll be using Guzzle[1] as my HTTP client and demonstrating a few calls for each of the highlighted APIs. With these expectations in mind, you should get a really good understanding for how to make these API calls.

Remember to install Guzzle with Composer:

```
composer require guzzlehttp/guzzle
```

This chapter will also highlight examples of other software which can be used to create OAuth 2.0 Clients and Servers. There will be examples and links to these projects to help get an understanding of how these work. All this is an attempt to more completely understand the options available.

[1]   https://github.com/guzzle/guzzle

Existing Libraries

One of our goals as creators of software should be to avoid reimplementing solutions for problems that have already been solved well. Whether you are creating a new service or hoping to integrate an existing service into your project, it's important to have an understanding of what is out there and how to use it correctly. With that said, let's take a look a couple of interesting, useful OAuth 2.0 projects you can implement in your project.

PHPLeague OAuth 2.0 Client

The first library I'm going to discuss is the OAuth 2.0 Client, https://github.com/thephpleague/oauth2-client, maintained by Ben Ramsey, which is part of The PHP League. This library provides mechanisms for retrieving an access token and using a refresh token, enabling you to make requests to third party services. The providers available to this client are maintained in separate repositories and include:

- Facebook, https://github.com/thephpleague/oauth2-facebook
- GitHub, https://github.com/thephpleague/oauth2-github
- Google, https://github.com/thephpleague/oauth2-google
- Instagram, https://github.com/thephpleague/oauth2-instagram
- LinkedIn, https://github.com/thephpleague/oauth2-linkedin

The PHP League OAuth 2.0 Client also provides some options when it comes to grants, allowing this package to be used for single page JavaScript applications, applications that utilize PHP Frameworks, as well as options for internal applications. The grants shipped with this package are as follows:

- Authorization Code Grant
- Refresh Token Grant
- Client Credentials Grant
- Resource Owner Grant

Also worth noting, this project has a full suite of unit tests and is available for install via Composer at the command line

```
composer require league/oauth2-client:~0.3
```

Or in your composer.json file:

```
{
    "require": {
        "league/oauth2-client": "~0.3"
    }
}
```

This project is hosted on GitHub[2]. The README is full of documentation on how to use the client, so rather than duplicate the information here, please visit the repository on GitHub to review the source code and documentation.

[2]   https://github.com/thephpleague/oauth2-client

Apigility

Apigility is a product from Zend Framework which allows you to create robust APIs very quickly. Apigility provides a GUI interface for everything you'd need to do when creating an API, including providing OAuth 2.0 authentication. Apigility is created in way that the Resource Server and Authentication server are delivered from the same API server. This is incredibly useful if you need to get an OAuth 2.0 API up and running quickly, as it will handle the creation of tokens, management of tokens, and the validation of tokens passed to the server. You can find more information about Apigility at http://www.apigility.org.

PHPLeague OAuth 2.0 Server

The other library I really wanted to highlight is from Alex Bilbie and compliments the OAuth 2.0 Client very well; it's the OAuth 2.0 Server. This server allows you to implement an OAuth 2.0 server very easily and is very well documented. This is another case where I'm going to refer you to the documentation (because it's good) and very specifically point out if you need an OAuth 2.0 server, this is a very strong choice.

One of the main differences and deciding factors for choosing between Apigility and OAuth 2.0 Server is availability of options. If you've written an API and are looking to move to OAuth 2.0 for auth, OAuth 2.0 Server will fit nicely with your existing API. If you have yet to build your API, Apigility provides a friendly interface allowing you to create the API and use OAuth 2.0 for authentication.

Service Providers

This section contains examples of using OAuth 2.0 to connect with service providers. I am going to provide a very general script which can be used to request and retrieve the tokens from these service providers. If there are differences between services, I will call those out at the beginning of each section.

To get started, let's a take a look at a basic script which allows us to retrieve our access token via the Authorization Code grant.

Listing 8.1

```
01. <?php
02. /**
03.  * First, direct the user to the authorize endpoint and this script acts as our callback.
04.  *
05.  * The authorize endpoint will have some parameters. Typically you'll need:
06.  *     https://<service url>/<oauth endpoint>?client_id=<client_token>&response_type=code
07.  *         &redirect_uri=http://thepath.to/this/script
08.  *
09.  * Tokens are saved in a session. You can run it with PHP's dev server:
10.  *     php -S http://127.0.0.1:8080/
11.  */
12.
13. require ('vendor/autoload.php');
14. session_start();
```

```
15.
16.  // Service specific configuration here
17.  $client_key = 'YOUR APPLICATION KEY';
18.  $client_secret = 'YOUR APPLICATION SECRET';
19.  $token_url = "https://<service url>/<oauth endpoint>";
20.  // you may need to whitelist the redirect_uri
21.  $redirect_uri = 'http://127.0.0.1:8080/';
22.
23.  if (isset($_GET['code'])) {
24.      // this is going to build the access token endpoint
25.      $params = [
26.          'client_id' => $client_key,
27.          'client_secret' => $client_secret,
28.          'grant_type' => 'authorization_code',
29.          'code' => $_GET['code'],
30.          'redirect_uri' => $redirect_uri,
31.      ];
32.
33.      $client = new \GuzzleHttp\Client();
34.      $response = $client->get($token_url . '?' . http_build_query($params));
35.      // Your access token will be part of the body returned by this endpoint,
36.      // typically via json.
37.      $json = $response->getBody()->getContents();
38.      $body = json_decode($json);
39.      // After this is where you would persist this token in a database or session.
40.      $_SESSION['access_token'] = $body->access_token;
41.      exit;
42.  }
43.
44.  // If we don't have a code, we need to request one. This section needs to be
45.  // customized per service.
46.  $auth_url = "https://<service url>/<authorize endpoint>";
47.  $params = [
48.      'client_id' => $client_key,
49.      'redirect_uri' => $redirect_uri,
50.  ];
51.  $auth_url .= "?" . http_build_query($params);
52.  Header("Location: {$auth_url}");
```

As always, you should check your API documentation to verify exactly how to build the endpoints for that service, but this is a pretty full example of the things you may need.

Foursquare

Foursquare is one of the most popular location based social networks around. Users can use their GPS-enabled smart phone to "check-in" at different locations. Some of the locations even have deals available once you check-in to their location. There's a wealth of data here, so it only makes sense that there's a way to retrieve and analyze it, right?

First, you need to create a new app on Foursquare at https://foursquare.com/developers/apps. The sign up form, which lists the access token and authorize URLs on the left, is shown in Figure 8.1. Once saved, the *Administrative Information* section of your application will have your Client ID and Client secret.

FIGURE 8.1

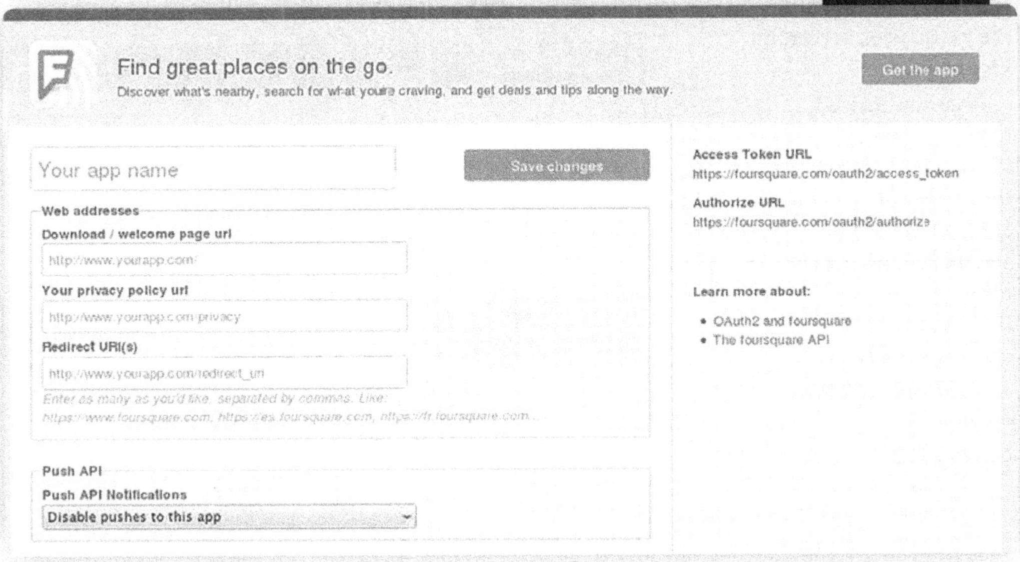

Foursquare has a public API built on the OAuth 2.0 Authorization Framework. It allows you to retrieve and create information for users, venues, check-ins, tips, lists and more. You'll need to retrieve an access token, as outlined in Listing 8.1.

The service specific configuration for Foursquare should be replaced with:

```
// Service specific configuration here
$client_key = 'YOUR KEY';
$client_secret = 'YOUR SECRET';
$token_url = 'https://foursquare.com/oauth2/access_token';
// assumes this file is index.php
$redirect_uri = 'http://127.0.0.1:8080/';
```

To redirect users to the authorization dialog on Foursquare, the end of the script should look like:

```
$auth_url = "https://foursquare.com/oauth2/authenticate";
$params = [
    'client_id' => $client_key,
    'response_type' => 'code',
    'redirect_uri' => $redirect_uri,
];
$auth_url .= "?" . http_build_query($params);
Header("Location: {$auth_url}");
```

When a user first navigates to your script, they will be presented with the permission screen in Figure 8.2.

Once authorized, Listing 8.2 will retrieve all the recent check-ins for the people you have connected with on Foursquare. There's a wealth of information available in these check-ins and you can use the data to create a pretty nifty looking display.

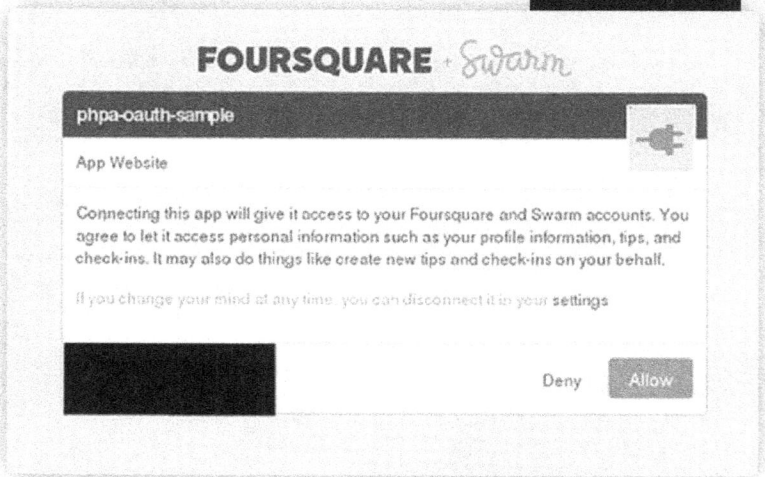

FIGURE 8.2

Listing 8.2

```
01. <?php
02. require ('vendor/autoload.php');
03. session_start();
04.
05. // prepare our endpoint
06. $endpoint = 'https://api.foursquare.com/v2/checkins/recent';
07. $params = [
08.     'oauth_token' => $_SESSION['access_token'],
09.     // There is a 'v' value that we have to supply as a yyyymmdd to indicate the expected
10.     // API version. If omitted, the request will be rejected
11.     'v' => '20140627'
12. ];
13. $endpoint .= '?' . http_build_query($params);
14.
15. $client = new \GuzzleHttp\Client();
16. $response = $client->get($endpoint);
17. $json = $response->getBody()->getContents();
```

```
18.  // this will decode the json into an array
19.  $data = json_decode($json, true);
20.
21.  // If you want to use the photo, you must request a size for the picture. The photo URI
22.  // information comes to us nicely, so here's how you'd request a 200x200 picture to use.
23.  $recent_checkins = $data['response']['recent'];
24.
25.  // let's loop through all the checkins and output the user photos and shouts
26.  foreach ($recent_checkins as $checkin) {
27.      // the shout
28.      echo "<h2>" . htmlentities($checkin['shout'], ENT_QUOTES) . "</h2>";
29.      echo "<h3> at " . htmlentities($checkin['venue']['name'], ENT_QUOTES) . "</h3>";
30.      // the user's photo
31.      $photo = $checkin['user']['photo']['prefix'];
32.      $photo .= '200x200';
33.      $photo .= $checkin['user']['photo']['suffix'];
34.
35.      echo '<img src="' . $photo '">';
36.  }
```

Since we have an example of how to read data from the Foursquare API, let's see if we can write a quick little script that allowing us to create a check-in. The `checkin/add` endpoint requires we send a POST request with some data in the request body. Let's see what this looks like, as you'll see in Listing 8.3, there's really not much to it.

Listing 8.3

```
01.  <?php
02.  /**
03.   * This script is going to allow us to checkin at a venue via the Foursquare API. In this
04.   * example, the venue id is known; but the venue end point can easily retrieve those
05.   * values if you don't know them.
06.   */
07.  require ('vendor/autoload.php');
08.  session_start();
09.
10.  // prepare our endpoint
11.  $endpoint = 'https://api.foursquare.com/v2/checkins/add';
12.  $params = [
13.      'oauth_token' => $_SESSION['access_token'],
14.      // There is a 'v' value that we have to supply as a yyyymmdd to indicate the expected
15.      // API version. If omitted, the request will be rejected
16.      'v' => '20140627'
17.  ];
18.  $endpoint .= '?' . http_build_query($params);
19.
20.  // for example sake, we're going to assume we already have the venue ID (RFK Stadium)
21.  $venue_id = '4b15505bf964a5206c1023e3';
```

```
22.
23. $client = new \GuzzleHttp\Client();
24. $response = $client->post( $endpoint, [
25.        'form_params' => [
26.            'shout' => 'I was here',
27.            'venueId' => $venue_id,
28.        ]
29. ]);
```

More information, including all the existing endpoints for the Foursquare API can be found at: https://developer.foursquare.com

GitHub

GitHub has exploded in popularity as a way to share code and projects with the world at large. Based on the popular Distributed Version Control System, git, GitHub allows developers spread all over the world to work closely together on projects. While it's great for dispersed teams, it's also widely used at companies where all the developers are local, due to the way it handles the integration of new code into projects.

FIGURE 8.3

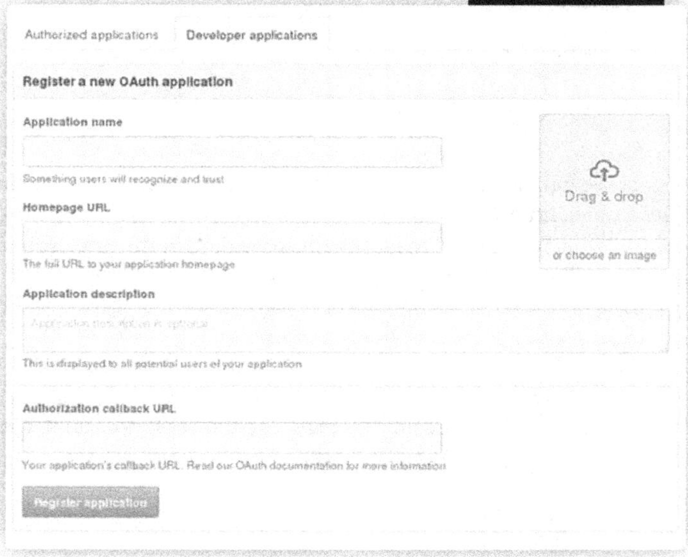

To register an application to use GitHub's OAuth integration, visit https://github.com/settings/applications/new. Figure 8.3 shows the registration form.

GitHub introduces a few new concepts in the way the request tokens are retrieved, so I've included some code demonstrating how to use the state and scopes option. If you recall, state acts as a kind of CSRF token and the scopes allow you to set the areas of the API the token can access. Listing 8.4 shows how you would go about getting the access token with GitHub.

Listing 8.4

```php
01. <?php
02. require_once 'vendor/autoload.php';
03. session_start();
04.
05. $client_id = 'YOUR ID';
06. $client_secret = 'YOUR SECRET';
07. $redirect_uri = 'http://127.0.0.1:8080';
08.
09. $scope = 'gist,user,repo';
10. $state = 'bbc434234cdcdc3423432';
11. $client = new \GuzzleHttp\Client();
12.
13. if (!isset($_GET['code'])) {
14.     $uri = 'https://github.com/login/oauth/authorize';
15.     $params = [
16.         'client_id' => $client_id,
17.         'redirect_uri' => $redirect_uri,
18.         'scope' => $scope,
19.         'state' => $state,
20.     ];
21.     $uri .= '?' . http_build_query($params);
22.     header("Location: $uri");
23.     exit;
24. }
25.
26. $endpoint = "https://github.com/login/oauth/access_token";
27. $code = $_GET['code'];
28. // if the states don't match stop!
29. if ($state !== $_GET['state']) {
30.     trigger_error('CSRF Detected!', E_USER_ERROR);
31. }
32.
33. $response = $client->post($endpoint, [
34.     'form_params' => [
35.         'client_id' => $client_id,
35.         'client_secret' => $client_secret,
37.         'code' => $code,
38.         'redirect_uri' => $redirect_uri
39.     ]
40. ]);
41. $body = $response->getBody()->getContents();
42.
43. // parse_str will parse the response body into the array $tokens. It will now hold the
44. // value of the 'access_token'
45. parse_str($body, $tokens);
46.
47. $_SESSION['access_token'] = $tokens['access_token'];
```

As you can see, the flow is pretty much the same, we've just added a few components. Now that we have our shiny, new access token, let's use it to get some information. Let's say we want to get a list of all the repositories we own. Assuming we've added the repo scope to our scopes list during the request process, we can do this very simply, see Listing 8.5.

Listing 8.5

```
01. <?php
02. require_once 'vendor/autoload.php';
03. session_start();
04.
05. $access_token = $_SESSION['access_token'];
06.
07. $client = new \GuzzleHttp\Client();
08. $response = $client->get("https://api.github.com/user/repos", [
09.     'headers'=> [
10.         'Accept' => 'application/vnd.github.v3+json',
11.         'Authorization' => "token {$access_token}"
12.     ]
13. ]);
14. $body = json_decode($response->getBody(), true);
15.
16. foreach ($body as $repo) {
17.     echo htmlentities($repo['name'], ENT_QUOTES) . ' '
18.         . htmlentities($repo['full_name'], ENT_QUOTES) . '<br>';
19. }
```

The script will print the name and full name of every repository we own, both public and private. If we wanted to keep our private repos out of the list we could add a query string to the URL ?type=public. If we wanted only our private repos we could use ?type=private. If we wanted to see just the repos we owned, add ?type=owner. There are sorting options as well; we can sort by created, update, pushed, and full name. You can check out https://developer.github.com/v3/repos for more information on how to interact with repositories.

Again, we've seen how simple it is to retrieve data from the API, but how about writing it? Let's take a look at a new concept and actually edit a gist. GitHub is good about using the proper HTTP methods, so we can see how a PATCH request would work. For the next example, you'll need to create a simple gist with a file name of oauth-gist.txt and some plain text content. Once created, the ID for the gist is the last component in the URL, for example:

https://gist.github.com/mfrost503/847dc6c4ea66f4fa037b

Now we can update it programatically, as shown in Listing 8.6.

Listing 8.6

```
01. <?php
02. require_once 'vendor/autoload.php';
03. session_start();
04.
05. $access_token = $_SESSION['access_token'];
06.
07. // ID of a gist that we can modify
08. $gist_id = 'e11aa9a8f4fc6b3de≥80';
09.
10. // prepare data for our patch
11. $data = [
12.     'description' => 'Updated Text',
13.     'files' => [
14.         'oauth-gist.txt' => [ 'content' => 'This is completely new text, right?' ]
15.     ]
16. ];
17.
18. // make the request
19. $client = new \GuzzleHttp\Client();
20. $response = $client->patch('https://api.github.com/gists/' . $gist_id, [
21.     'headers' => [
22.         'Accept' => 'application/vnd.github.v3+json',
23.         'Authorization' => "token $access_token"
24.     ],
25.     'body' => json_encode($data)
26. ]);
27.
28. // examine the response
29. $headers = $response->getHeaders();
30. echo "Status: " . $headers['Status'][0] . "<br />";
31.
32. $contents = $response->getBody()->getContents();
33. var_dump(json_decode($contents));
```

As you can see, editing gists is a pretty easy process. You can use this PATCH call to rename files and also create new files, but you only need to send what you want to change, not the whole resource. If you were to use a completely new file name, a gist with that file name, description, and contents would be created.

So there you have it, a quick dive into the GitHub API, you can probably already notice some differences between the GitHub API and the Foursquare API. I assure you there more differences coming, but that said, both APIs are extremely easy to work with. If you'd like to learn about the GitHub API and some of the awesome things you can do with it, check out https://developer.github.com/v3/

Instagram

With the increasing popularity of the "selfie", it's good to know there is a service which allows

FIGURE 8.4

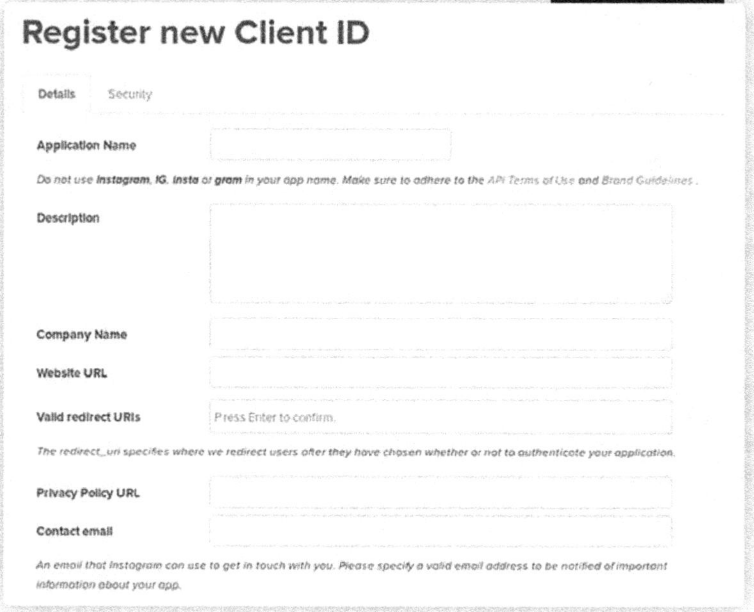

you to upload, host, and share all your images. Instagram provides an API which allows users to view media, retrieve information, and comment on other media. The access token is very similar to the very first example provided, so we will not go through that again.

To register a new application on Instagram, go to https://www.instagram.com/developer/clients/manage/. You'll see a form as shown in Figure 8.4.

We can reuse Listing 8.1 to get an access token to work with Instagram. The flow should be familiar; the main thing to note is Instagram requires a POST request to retrieve the access token. The updated script is shown in Listing 8.5.

Listing 8.7

```php
34. <?php
35. /**
36.  * Flow for getting an Authentication Token for an Instagram User.
37.  *
38.  * We will save tokens in a session. You can run it with PHPp's dev server:
39.  *     php -S http://127.0.0.1:8080/
40.  */
41. require ('vendor/autoload.php');
42. session_start();
43.
44. // Service specific configuration here
45. $client_key = 'YOUR APPLICATION ID';
46. $client_secret = 'YHOUR APPLICATION SECRET';
47.
48. // you may need to whitelist the redirect_uri
49. $redirect_uri = 'http://127.0.0.1:8080/';
50.
51. if (isset($_GET['code'])) {
52.     $client = new \GuzzleHttp\Client();
53.
54.     // unlike other services, Instagram requires a POST
55.     $response = $client->post('https://api.instagram.com/oauth/access_token', [
56.         'form_params' => [
57.             'client_id' => $client_key,
58.             'client_secret' => $client_secret,
59.             'grant_type' => 'authorization_code',
60.             'code' => $_GET['code'],
61.             'redirect_uri' => $redirect_uri,
62.         ]
63.     ]);
64.     // Your access token will be part of the body returned by this endpoint, via json.
65.     $json = $response->getBody()->getContents();
66.     $body = json_decode($json);
67.     // After this is where you would persist this token in a database or session.
68.     $_SESSION['access_token'] = $body->access_token;
69.     exit;
70. }
71.
72. // If we don't have a code, we need to request one.
73. $auth_url = "https://api.instagram.com/oauth/authorize/";
74. $params = [
75.     'client_id' => $client_key,
76.     'redirect_uri' => $redirect_uri,
77.     'response_type' => 'code',
78. ];
79. $auth_url .= "?" . http_build_query($params);
80. Header("Location: {$auth_url}");
```

Users will be shown a screen like the one in Figure 8.5 to authorize your application.

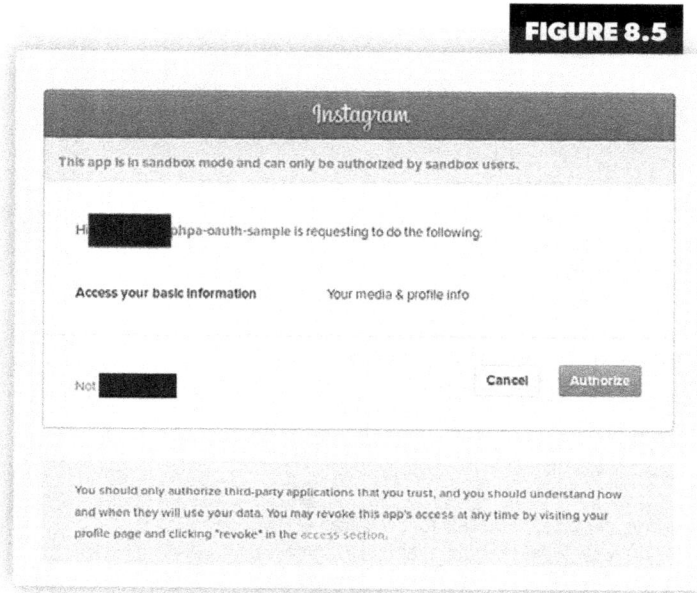

FIGURE 8.5

Now that we have a valid token, we can see in Listing 8.8 how to retrieve some basic information about the user, including their profile photo.

Listing 8.8

```php
01. <?php
02. require_once 'vendor/autoload.php';
03.
04. session_start();
05. $access_token = $_SESSION['access_token'];
06.
07. $client = new \GuzzleHttp\Client();
08.
09. $api = 'https://api.instagram.com/v1';
10. $url = $api . '/users/self/access_token=' . $access_token;
11.
12. $response = $client->get($url);
13. $body = $response->getBody()->getContents();
14. $user = json_decode($body);
15.
16. echo '<h1>' . htmlentities($user->data->username, ENT_QUOTES) . '</h1>';
17.
18. echo '<img src="' . $user->data->profile_picture . '">';
```

Simple, right? Next, we would normally do a follow up on how to create content, however, in an effort to not annoy a ton of people by liking, disliking, and commenting on photos, let's not do that with this particular service. What I'm going to do here instead, is provide a more complex example to actually pull some media, see Listing 8.9. As always, you can explore the API documentation more after the fact if commenting is something you have an interest in doing.

Listing 8.9

```php
01. <?php
02. require_once 'vendor/autoload.php';
03.
04. session_start();
05. $access_token = $_SESSION['access_token'];
06.
07. $client = new \GuzzleHttp\Client();
08. $base_url = "https://api.instagram.com/v1/";
09.
10. // Let's retrieve a list of our followers and look at the most recent media from our
11. // first follower.
12.
13. $follower_uri = $base_url . 'users/self/followed-by?access_token=' . $access_token;
14.
15. $follow_response = $client->get($follower_uri);
16. $followers = json_decode($follow_response->getBody()->getContents(), true);
17. $follower_id = $followers['data'][1]['id'];
18.
19. $recentmedia_uri = $base_url . 'users/' . $follower_id . '/media/recent?access_token='
20.     . $access_token;
21.
22. $recentmedia_response = $client->get($recentmedia_uri);
23. $recentmedia = json_decode($recentmedia_response->getBody()->getContents(), true);
24. $recentmedia_id = $recentmedia['data'][0]['id'];
25.
26. $media_uri = $base_url . 'media/' . $recentmedia_id . '?access_token=' . $access_token;
27. $media_response = $client->get($media_uri);
28. $media = json_decode($media_response->getBody()->getContents(), true);
29. print $media['data']['user']['full_name'];
```

As you might imagine, there is far more data regarding the actual media available after the media call. You can get information about the user, links, dimensions for different resolutions of the photo, the comments, and–of course–the likes. I would encourage you to take a look at http://instagram.com/developer if you would like more information about what's available in this API.

Reddit

Reddit is a social news network which allows registered users to post content, links, and other types of content. The users can then vote a thread up or down. People can build reputation based on how popular their posts tend to be. There's a large contingency of programmers using Reddit regularly, but there are topics for many different interests.

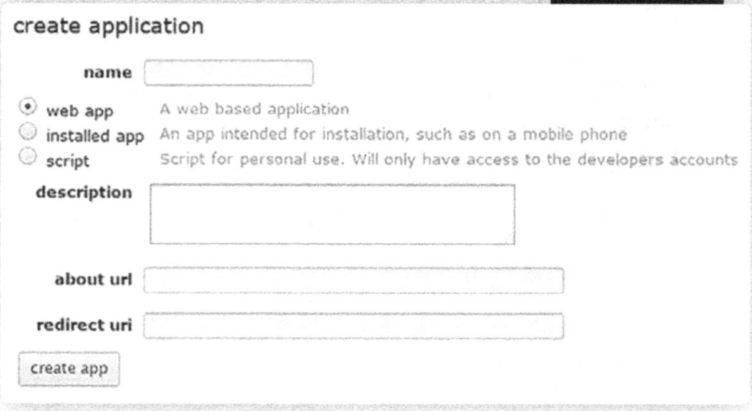

FIGURE 8.6

To register an application to use Reddit's OAuth support, start by visiting https://www.reddit.com/prefs/apps. Clicking on the *are you a developer? create an app...* button brings up the form shown in Figure 8.6.

The token process for Reddit is quite a bit different from anything we've seen. While the core of the process remains the same, there are a couple of different things we have to do to make the request. Listing 9 is a script we can use to get these tokens. In it, we will see how to use Basic Auth to authorize the access token request.

Listing 8.10

```php
01. <?php
02. require_once 'vendor/autoload.php';
03. session_start();
04.
05. $client_key = 'YOUR APPLICATION KEY';
06. $client_secret = 'YOUR APPLICATION SECRET';
07. $state = 'abvder2343fsdfewr';
08. $duration = 'permanent';
09. $scope = 'flair,history,read,vote,identity';
10. $redirect_uri = 'http://oauth.dev:8080/';
11.
12. if (!isset($_GET['code'])) {
13.     $url = 'https://ssl.reddit.com/api/v1/authorize';
14.     $params = [
15.         'client_id' => $client_id,
16.         'response_type' => 'code',
17.         'state' => $state,
18.         'redirect_uri' => $redirect_uri,
19.         'scope' => $scope,
20.     ];
```

```
21.    $url .= '?' . http_build_query($params);
22.    header("Location: $url");
23.    exit;
24. }
25.
26. $client = new \GuzzleHttp\Client();
27. // create basic authentication with client id and client secret
28. $basicAuth = base64_encode("{$client_id}:{$client_secret}");
29.
30. $response = $client->post('https://ssl.reddit.com/api/v1/access_token', [
31.    'headers' => [ 'Authorization' => 'Basic ' . $basicAuth ],
32.    'form_params' => [
33.       'grant_type' => 'authorization_code',
34.       'code' => $_GET['code'],
35.       'redirect_uri' => $redirect_uri,
36.    ]
37. ]);
38. $body = $response->getBody()->getContents();
39. $tokens = json_decode($body);
40. $_SESSION['access_token'] = $tokens->access_token;
```

It's important to pay attention to the scopes. Many of the endpoints are scoped and there are quite a few to pick from. It's a good idea to get acquainted with them before making the request for the tokens. When a user is authorizing your application, they'll see them in the approval dialog, as in Figure 8.7.

FIGURE 8.7

The example I'm going to show for Reddit is the retrieval of your own user information, which requires the identity scope, see Listing 8.11.

Listing 8.11

```
01. <?php
02. require ('vendor/autoload.php');
03. session_start();
04. $access_token = $_SESSION['access_token'];
05.
06. try {
07.     $client = new \GuzzleHttp\Client();
08.     $response = $client->get('https://oauth.reddit.com/api/v1/me', [
09.         'headers' => [ 'Authorization' => 'bearer ' . $access_token ]
10.     ]);
11.
12.     $response = $response->getBody()->getContents();
13.     var_dump($user);
14. } catch(\GuzzleHttp\Exception\ClientException $e) {
15.     echo $e->getMessage();
16. }
```

You can find more information about the Reddit API at http://www.reddit.com/dev/api

YouTube

YouTube is a Google product which hosts videos and offers them for viewing. The YouTube API is part of the Google API family and has libraries for a number of different languages. To get started, visit https://console.developers.google.com/start, and in the right pop-out menu click on *API Manager* to register an application. Once created, you'll need to create credentials for each API you want to use to get a secret.

While we're not going to get into those libraries specifically, we are able to write a script to provide us with an access token, see Listing 8.12. Most Google APIs function the same way and support OAuth 2.0[3]. Once you have the access token, you should be able to use it to access any of the APIs you've enabled in the Google API console.

[3]   https://developers.google.com/identity/protocols/OAuth2

Listing 8.12

```php
01. <?php
02. require_once 'vendor/autoload.php';
03.
04. $client_id = 'YOUR CLIENT ID';
05. $client_secret = 'YOUR CLIENT SECRET';
06. $redirect_uri = 'http://127.0.0.1:8080/';
07.
08. if (!isset($_GET['code'])) {
09.     $params = [
10.         'client_id' => $client_id,
11.         'redirect_uri' => $redirect_uri,
12.         'response_type' => 'code',
13.         'scope' => 'https://www.googleapis.com/auth/youtube',
14.         'access_type' => 'offline',
15.     ];
16.
17.     $auth_url = "https://accounts.google.com/o/oauth2/auth?" . http_build_query($params);
18.     header("Location: $auth_url");
19.     exit;
20. }
21.
22. $client = new \GuzzleHttp\Client();
23. $response = $client->post('https://accounts.google.com/o/oauth2/token', [
24.     'form_params' => [
25.         'client_id' => $client_id,
26.         'client_secret' => $client_secret,
27.         'redirect_uri' => $redirect_uri,
28.         'code' => $_GET['code'],
29.         'grant_type' => 'authorization_code',
30.     ]
31. ]);
32.
33. $body = $response->getBody()->getContents();
34. $tokens = json_decode($body);
35.
36. $_SESSION['access_token'] = $tokens->access_token;
37. $_SESSION['refresh_token'] = $tokens->refresh_token;
```

This pretty much sums up how to use any of the Google APIs, the following links that will help you learn more about the libraries and how to use them. Google has the most concepts to get familiar with from what we've seen here. This is due to the way Google has packaged their family of APIs. If you are interested in checking out the Google APIs, head over to https://developers.google.com. You can browse the APIs and read documentation about each one. You can check out the Developers console at https://console.developers.google.com; this is where you can setup a new project and configure your callbacks.

Conclusion

This chapter provides a good jumping off point for working with some of these APIs and gives you a nice practical application for retrieving tokens and hitting end points with Guzzle. A lot of the code was written in a way which makes the functionality extremely obvious, so keep that in mind if you actually use some of these examples. There are optimizations and security concerns you need to consider. I hope these examples clarified the practical questions you have and have encouraged you to take on OAuth 2.0 APIs in your projects.

Chapter

9

Security

Nothing will scare away your users like an insecure application. Regardless of how many cool bells and whistles you have, when users fear for the safety and privacy of their information they are likely to head towards the hills. In fact, they may even like your application so much they decide to develop a competing product, without the security holes. We've discussed a lot of really great information up to this point and we've seen how easy it is to integrate popular services into our own web applications through APIs. It's important we not lose sight of the fact we are acting on behalf of the user and often handling some very important, sensitive, and private information for these users.

We've discussed at great length how dangerous passing user credentials through HTTP requests can be and how OAuth helps mitigate the risks involved. While using OAuth does eliminate some obvious security concerns, it is still important to keep security in mind when developing your API driven web application. This chapter will look at common security concerns when providing and consuming APIs and how we can take proper measures to protect our users.

Application Security

Integrating services into our web application allows us to create rich applications that open many doors for our users. Since we're acting on behalf of our users, there are certain things we need to make sure we do to avoid compromising security.

Token Security

One of the most convenient aspects of OAuth is the ability to allow the users to authenticate with the service they are hoping to use. They also have the ability to revoke access to your application at any point in time. When a user chooses to allow access to your application, you become responsible for handling the token associated to their account. In most cases, the user doesn't even know you are exchanging their authentication for a token. If a user has an account on an external services compromised, they'll often have to to through a process of selectively revoking the access other applications have to the compromised service.

There is some diversity in how you handle OAuth tokens, a good part of that depends on which version of OAuth you are using. It might make more sense with the longer lived tokens in OAuth 1.0 to persist these values in a database, while OAuth 2.0 tokens might make more sense to store in a session. Regardless of how you store them, it's important they stay within your application.

Stolen access tokens and client tokens can lead to a situation where another user can access the API on behalf of the authenticated user. To put it in different terms, an attacker would be able to "login" as another user on the service and access their account for reading, writing, updating, and deleting information. It's vitally important to store all credentials and tokens securely.

SQL Injection

SQL Injection is one of the more well known types of attacks and can be used access data that is persisted in a database. To be clear, the SQL Injection attack in this scenario would be against your application and not the service being used. A SQL Injection attack happens when data is inserted directly into an SQL query without being sanitized beforehand. The results can be disastrous and can vary based on the motives of the attacker.

When an SQL Injection attack is successfully executed, data can be deleted and additional data can be gathered from databases that should never be exposed to the outside world. Obviously, if you are persisting access tokens in the database, this can result in exposing all the stored access tokens to the attackers.

To mitigate these types of attacks, a best practice is to always use prepared statements. In PHP, extensions like PDO and MySQLi offer this functionality and it goes a long way in protecting your application and database. Another way to mitigate these attacks is to validate all input values every single time before querying the database. Validating can be as simple as understanding types of values you are expecting to get and abandoning the query if something different from what you expected is provided. Validation is a strong step in preventing attack data from even making it to your query. PHP's built-in `filter_var` and related functions can help here.

Lastly, it's very important you handle errors correctly. SQL errors that output to the browser provide a lot of information attackers can use to gain more information about your database and table structure. It's important to understand what happens when a query fails and ensure you aren't giving the attackers the ammunition they need to successfully attack you. The less an attacker knows and can discover about your stack and the software you are using, the more difficult it is for them to attack you and the more likely they move on to attacking easier targets.

File System Vulnerabilities

The one predictable thing about web applications is they run on a server and the server can access everything your application needs to run. It's important to understand how we structure our application on the file system. One of the major concerns is storing configurations in publicly accessible location or in the web root. When configurations and other information is accessible to the public, it can lead to database configurations and API Client Credentials being compromised.

> *The* Web Root *or* Document Root *is the directory from which your web server is configured to serve to requests.*

File system vulnerabilities can take different forms, and everything from configurations to session information can be stolen if your file system is improperly secured. When you are setting up a server for production use, it's important to understand the best way to secure your file system from attackers. This includes everything from what you put in the web root to where you store PHP sessions. If you are unsure of the best ways to do this securely, I would implore you to hire a security expert to assist you in getting your file system set up correctly. It might cost you up front, but it is money you can easily justify spending since recovering from a security breach can be more costly.

Access Control and Scopes

As the creator of an application it's important your access control is set up properly. Obviously, allowing authenticated users to see the private information of other users is not a situation you want to find yourself in. In addition to leaking presumably private user content, this can lead to an account being hijacked. It can also lead to the leaking of OAuth credentials.

Scopes are another important aspect of security related specifically to OAuth. It is important to only grant access to the set of scopes necessary for your application to function properly. Granting access to scopes your application isn't actively using is a very poor design choice. If OAuth credentials are hijacked, an attacker can gain access to parts of a third-party service they shouldn't have.

For example, if your integration with a service only requires you read data from the service, make sure you don't have scopes set allowing a user to write or delete data. Early in the application development cycle, you may be unsure of what scopes your user should be authorized to use. In this case, it is important to selectively add and remove scopes throughout the process. It's a topic that should be revisited often and have adjustments made as necessary. Every scope you include should be justifiable in the context of your application. If you find your scope needs to change after you have authenticated users, generating new access tokens is a relatively trivial task, you should do this when necessary.

Social Engineering

There are certainly a lot of responsibilities that fall to application developers when it comes to securing user data. There are also some very important things to be aware of if you are using an application. While the movies might portray computer hacking as a highly technical endeavor, a lot of information is given away for free in social engineering attacks. Some of these attacks can be highly technical, such as phishing or spoofing, while others are as simple as a phone call or email.

To this point, a vast majority of the information provided is centered around application developers securing data; it is vitally important we know how to protect ourselves as well as users. This section is going to focus solely on ways we can protect our information and should hopefully raise our sense of awareness on how other people may try to get information from us.

Phishing

Fraud and stealing user data can be very lucrative; it's one of the reasons so many attackers will go to great lengths to trick us into giving up sensitive information. A phishing attack happens when an attacker poses as a credible business, or perhaps even the service we are using in order to make us feel comfortable about giving them information.

Often times phishing websites spend a great deal of time and care in making their application look very similar to another service in order to fool users. They trick visitors into thinking they are providing their credentials or API information for completely legitimate purposes such as updating account information or verifying an account is still active. In some cases, they may even tell us they need our information because our account suffered a security breach and users need to re-verify their identities. This works, with alarming frequency, because it sounds legitimate and users will do anything to protect themselves and their data. Little do users know, the attack is actually being carried out as he or she types their username and password into the provided fields.

A lot of services have gone out of their way to include phrases like "We'll never ask you for your credentials" in their emails. This is helpful when users are deciding whether to fill out that form or not. While the majority of these attacks are looking for usernames and passwords, don't rule out the possibility of one of these attacks targeting Access Keys and/or access secrets. Right now, it's not the main attack vector, but over time you may find attackers looking for that very information.

Spotting a phishing attack can be tricky at first, especially when they've done a good job replicating the look and feel of the application. You may actually be familiar with the graphics, layout, and wording on the spoofed website. To mitigate this attack, it's always important to check the

URL shown in the browser location bar. If the URL doesn't contain the hostname of the service you are using, it's probably fake. If you have any doubt in your mind about whether the site is legitimate, you're better off closing it and not providing the requested information. You should also be able to email the support staff at the service, as they will likely be aware of the company's policy of asking you to provide your credentials.

Phone Calls and Emails

When done badly this type of attack is really obvious to detect. The problem is the successful attackers aren't bad at it. Attackers are keen at getting whatever little information they can, and they know how to use it to their full advantage. If someone were to call you and ask for your username, password, access token, etc. you would hopefully have enough sense to not share it information with them.

What if someone called as a representative of MySQL and asked you to take a quick phone survey regarding your satisfaction with the product? If you are willing to offer up the information, you might reveal you are in fact using the product, what version of the product you are using, and maybe even some details about how you are using the product. All this information could be extremely valuable to attackers and it may give them the information they need to successfully execute an attack on your application or probe further. A good piece of advice when dealing with "vendor" calls is to avoid giving out any information on the phone and letting your superiors know the call was made. Never give out information to people that have called you seeking it. A survey may seem like a legitimate reason for a call, but keep in mind, that is what makes the attack so successful.

User IDs

For a while using auto-incrementing integers was all the rage when it came to identifying users internally. As we've learned, this provides a lot of information to would-be attackers and gives them a much better understanding how our data is structured. As we've seen, we should not be giving attackers any sort of information. For example, if you somehow expose user IDs in a URL, an attacker can discern how many users you have by simply incrementing the user ID until they receive a **404 Not Found** status. This can be used by attackers to scout whether your application is worth the time and effort it takes to attack. While this might not seem like a huge deal if you run a pretty a small application, I'm going to assume most applications are developed with an intent on being popular and well-used.

The other danger in this regard is it allows attackers to collect data on every user in your database by incrementing the ID number We certainly strive to make our applications as user and developer friendly as possible, but we stand to reveal a lot of information in this model. A better application security practice is to generate random hashes for each user and to use them in place of auto-incrementing integers as external identifiers. These random hashes are just that–random. They are not hashes of the auto-incrementing integers and they are not hashes of a combination of easily retrieved data; they are randomly generated.

```
$id = md5(openssl_random_pseudo_bytes(128));
```

By using hashes, we gain more control over our application and keep very important information close to the vest. Auto-incrementing ID's are often used because they are much easier to generate, required by the database, and essentially do the work for us. I would encourage you to take the steps necessary to move away from integer IDs to using hashes or to plan on using hashes in a new application. Security isn't always the most time-efficient practice, but any attempt at keeping our data away from attackers is time well spent. Any information the users need to know should be made known to the users appropriately. If you can't answer "Why would a user need this information?", they very well may not need it at all.

Token Expiration

Throughout the book we've learned how access credentials are generated. With a little practice this becomes quite trivial. There's always a concern that by requesting new tokens we are bothering the user or degrading the user experience of our application. There's a very fine line we walk between security and user experience, and it's important to err on the side of security as much as humanly possible.

Tokens, as we know, can be stolen and obtained through nefarious means. It's imperative we have a way to revoke those tokens when they are stolen. It's also important we not let them sit around forever. A design feature which makes OAuth far more secure than passing our credentials across the Web is the fact they are only valid with the client credentials we're using. This means the lifted tokens do not provide carte blanche access to all of our information in any context. While this is good, our credentials are handed over to us for a very specific reason. access secret was given that name for a very particular reason–it's supposed to be a secret. It's quite possible our tokens have been stolen and we've not been able to see the full effects of this thievery yet, but what is important is that we have some way to invalidate them.

The most practical way to invalidate tokens is to expire them. Once they've existed beyond the predetermined amount of time, they become utterly useless. This is one of the scenarios which might cause us somewhat of a usability concern, but rest assured, an access token can be obtained or refreshed in a way that's not intrusive. When a token expires, any request sent using that token should be unsuccessful. An expired token could lead to an Unauthorized status from the server and serve as notice to make a request for a new access token.

The OAuth 2.0 specification makes several mentions of access token expiration, which indicates that while an attack vector may be hard to visualize, generating new tokens on a regular basis is a good practice. In the long run, it's a situation where we should focus on the service and security we're providing to the user instead of focusing on the the time we're spending to implement the solution. Security is never easy, but invalidating tokens regularly you gain some peace of mind, and decrease the likelihood stolen tokens will lead to the compromise of your user's data.

Conclusion

This chapter explored many different ways our data can be compromised. While not all of them relate directly to OAuth as a protocol, some of these attacks can be used in tandem to cause us problems. It's important to point out we should be writing software with security as a primary concern in our mind. This chapter about security is by no means exhaustive when you consider all the ways attackers try to manipulate and steal our data. I highly suggest investigating the topic thoroughly before you start working on your next application. You should also have a security audit performed on any existing codebase to identify vulnerabilities, and so you can take the necessary steps to protect your users.

Whether we're writing or integrating web services, it's important to remember we as developers are in charge of security. It's not up to anyone else. If we aren't looking out for our users and our data, I guarantee no one else is either. Security is not a bolted-on feature. Rather, it is a mindset we must always be in so we can provide secure, useful software. If nothing else, this chapter should open your eyes to the vital task that lies in front of you as you build your applications.

SECURITY

www.ingramcontent.com/pod-product-compliance
Lightning Source LLC
Chambersburg PA
CBHW051223200326

41519CB00025B/7232